# NEW RULES
# OF
# RETIREMENT

# NEW RULES OF RETIREMENT

## WHAT YOUR FINANCIAL ADVISOR ISN'T TELLING YOU

# WARREN A. MACKENZIE AND KEN HAWKINS

Collins

*New Rules of Retirement*
© 2008 by Warren A. MacKenzie
and Ken Hawkins.
All rights reserved.

Published by Collins, an imprint of
HarperCollins Publishers Ltd

HarperCollins books may be purchased for
educational, business, or sales promotional
use through our Special Markets Department.

HarperCollins Publishers Ltd
2 Bloor Street East, 20th Floor
Toronto, Ontario, Canada
M4W 1A8

*www.harpercollins.ca*

Library and Archives Canada Cataloguing in
Publication information is available.

ISBN 978-1-55468-001-6

RRD 9 8 7 6 5 4 3 2 1
Printed and bound in the United States

Design by Sharon Kish

To my wife, Paulette—W.M.

To my father, Joe Hawkins—K.H.

# Contents

# Tables

# Introduction

As we were putting the finishing touches on this book, the United States housing market was collapsing, stock markets around the world were ricocheting, and millions of people in both Canada and the U.S. were nervously wondering what would happen to their retirement savings. One of our clients phoned me in a panic. With his planned retirement just a few years away, his multimillion-dollar portfolio, heavily weighted toward stocks, had lost 40 percent of its value in a matter of days. What was his advisor telling him to do? To stay the course—and to buy more stocks.

This example is hardly surprising. Sadly, it's the type of thing we see every day. In the financial services industry, the term "retirement planning" is either misused or misleading. A reasonable individual might think that this term means developing a plan for what to do when he or she is no longer working. In the financial services industry, however, "retirement planning" simply means developing a plan for saving and investing your money. Take a look at part of a recent advertisement from a major Canadian financial institution:

> INVESTMENT AND RETIREMENT PLANNERS
>
> Are you a sales-oriented, self-managed/motivated individual willing to work on 100% commission? We have exciting opportunities for Investment and Retirement Planners, so come join us!
>
> As a mobile, self-directed sales professional, you will meet with clients and promote products and services that meet their investment and retirement needs. The ideal candidates will have expertise in financial planning that has been gained through highly successful sales experience in the financial industry (minimum 2 years).

When you first read the job title in this ad, Investment and Retirement Planners, you might think that the recruiter is looking for individuals who are going to help clients plan for their retirement by reviewing and discussing many important retirement-related issues. In fact, what the recruiter is really looking for is salespeople to actively sell the funds and products of the financial institution that employs them. The new recruits will not be paid to do retirement planning, and no experience in retirement planning is required of them.

It may sound strange coming from two Bay Street veterans, but we believe retirement planning should start with the individual, not with his or her bank account. The traditional "financial planning" approach—retirement planning with a sole emphasis on assets, income, liability, and expenses—misses the bigger picture. Retirement planning (as it is normally understood) ignores our human assets or human capital and fails to include emotional and psychological preparation along with financial preparation.

Retirement is both a process and a life stage. In preparing for retirement, it is not enough to know how much money you will need, where you are going to live, or how you are going to spend your time. It is also necessary to understand that your attitudes, concerns, and emotions, as well as your financial needs, will change as you age.

The myth that is perpetuated in society in general, and in the financial services industry in particular, is that the higher your standard of living, the happier you will be. Therefore, the argument goes, the prime objective in retirement is to achieve the best standard of living possible by saving money while you are working and properly managing your wealth when you retire. The implication is that a high standard of living means a happy, successful, and fulfilling retirement.

The fact is, you need to have a broader perspective of retirement than a simply financial view will provide. A broad approach will help you set priorities, allowing you to put financial issues in their proper context and to gain a more fulfilling life. If you concentrate too much on the financial side of the planning exercise, you will end up focusing narrowly on financial security and standard of living, as if these were the only goals in retirement. While you are focusing on financial matters, you can easily overlook some of the other important elements that give meaning and enjoyment to life.

Planning and preparing for retirement is about taking control of your life, setting realistic goals, and making a plan to achieve them. It is about reducing the uncertainty surrounding your retirement. It involves asking questions, imagining different scenarios, considering different courses of action, and making decisions. Research confirms that people who plan properly and are financially and psychologically prepared have a better and more enjoyable retirement. By the way, avoiding the decision-making process does not mean you have not made a decision—rather, it means you've decided to give up control and let events carry you along.

In order to enjoy a successful retirement, you need the right preparation, the right expectations, and the right attitudes. By now you probably know that life is not a dress rehearsal; this is your last chance to enjoy all that you can enjoy. If you have another 30 years, use this time wisely by maximizing the potential for your happiness and for the happiness of those around you.

# Part 1
## Understand How Retirement Is Evolving

RETIREMENT AND OUR PERCEPTION OF RETIREMENT ARE RAPIDLY EVOLVING. WHEN OUR parents and grandparents retired, spending an entire career working for one company was the norm rather than the exception. On the day workers retired, they moved from a life dominated by work to a life of leisure. Retirement was considered the last phase of a life that could be divided neatly into three parts. The first 20 years was devoted to growing up and getting an education. The next period, of about 40 to 45 years, was devoted to working, supporting the family, and saving for retirement. The last period, which was not expected to be a long one, was devoted to leisure and sedentary activities.

Today we think of retirement not as retiring from life, but rather as entering a new and exciting phase of life. Retirees now have a greater life expectancy than their parents did and they see their retirement years very differently. In a recent survey by BMO Financial Group, 87 percent of respondents believed that the term "retirement" should be redefined. The top phrases they chose for a new definition were, "the next stage of my life," "the rest of my life," "the time to pursue my dreams," and "the second half of my life." Retirement now marks the beginning of a new life phase as opposed to merely the end of our working life.

Retirees of the last 10 to 20 years have been at the forefront of the changes taking place in retirement living. Compared to the previous generation, they are healthier, thanks to modern medicine, and wealthier, in part due to strong housing and stock markets since the early 1980s. Many of this generation of retirees took early retirement because of the incentives offered at work to make room for the baby boomers coming up behind them. Many retirees could afford to live where they wanted. Although most chose not to move, others downsized and moved to smaller communities with a more moderate climate and better way of living. These retirees developed active lifestyles and saw their retirement years as a time of personal growth. In the process, they changed our perception of retirement.

The first wave of baby boomers will turn 63 in 2009 and will collect Old Age Security in 2011. Many of these people have already retired. As this group ages, the growth in the number of seniors will be staggering. Those 65 and over made up 13.7 percent of the population in 2006, but this number is expected to rise to 21.2 percent by 2026. Researchers estimate that people age 60 and over will number 10.6 million by 2026, a growth of almost 4.8 million people over the 2006 figure. This number is greater than the population of Vancouver, Calgary, and Edmonton combined!

If you are a baby boomer, how will these numbers affect your own retirement? First, you can expect the economic and political power of your generation to continue. Companies will not be able to ignore the sheer size and growth of the seniors market and will develop new products to serve it. In the financial services industry over the past 20 years, products and services were designed to help investors accumulate wealth. Over the next 20 years, the products will be designed to begin distributing wealth, with retirement income in mind. In the real estate development industry, more and different types of housing will be available to seniors. This growing economic power will mean that additional options will be available to you in all aspects of your life—from health care to lifestyle choices to how to invest and spend your money.

Baby boomers are healthier, better educated, wealthier, less conservative and more technologically adept than their parents. They also believe they are not as old as their actual age. In a study done by The Strategic Counsel for *The Globe and Mail* in 2006, 55 percent of baby boomers age 50 to 59 thought of themselves as younger than their age and only 3 percent thought of themselves as older than their age. People who still believe themselves to be "young" are not going to "retire" as was traditionally known, but will instead remain very active in retirement.

Although retirement as we know it is evolving dramatically, many people contemplating it today have the same concerns as previous generations. Will I be able to maintain a reasonable standard of living? Will I run out of money before I die? Where will I live when I no longer have to work? How will I spend my leisure time? How can I be certain that my retirement will be enjoyable and relatively worry-free?

The options you have as you enter into this next phase of your life are greater than ever before. However, these additional options and choices do not always make decision making easier. You can have a more customized lifestyle but it might be more complicated. Your life might be more rewarding but at the same time more demanding. Additional choices and greater flexibility can complicate the process, making it more difficult to plan. More than ever, the key to a successful and fulfilling retirement is being armed with proper planning and preparation and the right information.

# Rule 1
## Throw Away the Old Retirement Myths

In planning for retirement, it is important to base your decisions on real facts, not conjecture, and on your unique circumstances rather than arbitrary rules of thumb or generalizations. Here are some of the myths about retirement perpetuated in society, in the media, or in advertising that we think should be debunked and thrown away.

### MYTH: RETIREMENT MEANS NOT WORKING

When the term "retirement" first came into use, someone who retired went suddenly from a life dominated by work to a life of leisure. The period of retirement was not expected to be significant in terms of the person's overall lifespan.

**REALITY:** Working during retirement is no longer an oxymoron. Individuals are starting to incorporate work into their retirement plans, not only to supplement income from other sources, but also for the satisfaction derived from work. What is different from before is that work will no longer be the main focus of people's lives. During retirement, work is secondary and must fit into a person's chosen lifestyle.

Today's retirees are more likely to phase in their retirement over a period that could last up to 15 years. During this period they might start a new career or business, work part-time, share a job with a colleague, or do some consulting. In short, work can be an important part of retirement and you should at least consider it as a possibility when you are working on your retirement plans.

### MYTH: RETIREMENT MEANS LIVING A LIFE OF LEISURE

Retirement is still viewed by some as a time for relaxing, travelling, golfing, puttering around the garden, or taking up hobbies. It is seen as time spent in leisure and idleness.

**REALITY:** Today's retirees are more likely to consider retirement as a time for regeneration rather than strictly as a time for winding down. It is a period to engage in meaningful activities, start a new business, go back for further education, or volunteer in the community. Retirement now means being actively engaged in life rather than retreating from it.

## MYTH: RETIREMENT IS STRICTLY AN ECONOMIC EVENT
The financial services industry wants you to believe that retirement is an event defined by money.

REALITY: Retirement is an economic event but it is also much more. It is a major life turning point, a time when we come to grips with our own mortality and realize we can no longer take our good health for granted. Retirement is also a significant psychological event, especially for those who have defined themselves by their work. It can be a time when we reinvent ourselves.

## MYTH: YOU CAN DETERMINE THE AGE AT WHICH YOU RETIRE
Most individuals approaching retirement believe they can pick their own retirement date and retire on their own terms. They believe that they can choose to retire at a certain age, say 65, when the government programs kick in, or that they can continue to work as long as they choose or until they have sufficient money to retire in comfort.

REALITY: In fact, many people have no control over their retirement date; it is chosen for them. Some people are forced to retire because of health reasons such as sudden illness, work injuries, or a body that has broken down from years of hard physical labour. Others must retire early to care for family members. Many others are forced into early retirement because of mandatory retirement policies or a corporate restructuring. Those who are forced out of their job when they are in their 50s or 60s are often unable to find another one and retire because there is no other work available. A recent Statistics Canada survey found that 27 percent of recently retired men and women had stopped working involuntarily. Of those, 44 percent had retired due to poor health, and 25 percent due to corporate downsizing.

## MYTH: RETIREES NEED 80 PERCENT OF THEIR PRE-RETIREMENT INCOME TO MAINTAIN THEIR STANDARD OF LIVING

This is one of those rules of thumb that are perpetuated by many people in the financial services industry and by those who provide retirement planning advice.

REALITY: The first flaw in this theory is that it doesn't take into account the general income level of those who are retiring. Individuals who have a high income pre-retirement generally need less, as a percentage of their previous income, than those with a lower level. For example, those with an annual family income of $150,000 with no mortgage or extra expenses might need only 40 percent of their pre-retirement income—$60,000—to maintain their standard of living, while those earning $30,000 might need 100 percent, or $30,000. Those who save a good portion of their income pre-retirement and lead very modest lifestyles might need only 50 percent of their income because in retirement they will not be putting aside money to fund their needs, and their taxes will be lower. Other people plan to spend over 100 percent of their pre-retirement income for at least the first few years in retirement to pay for the trip of a lifetime or other indulgences.

The second flaw in the myth is the assumption that people want to maintain the same standard of living in retirement that they enjoyed pre-retirement. In fact, many people will gladly accept a lower standard of living if it allows them to retire early.

The amount of income required for a satisfying retirement is based on unique needs and lifestyle choices, not on an arbitrary rule of thumb.

## MYTH: RETIREES NEED TO LIVE OFF THEIR INVESTMENT INCOMES WITHOUT TOUCHING THE PRINCIPAL

This myth leads many retirees to try to maximize the cash flow generated by their capital and causes many investors to take on higher levels of risk than necessary.

REALITY: Unless investors have a strong desire to leave an estate to their children or a charity, they can draw down their capital and use their principal as a source of funds to finance retirement. Purchasing an annuity with part of your capital is an easy way to use up capital while still ensuring that you never run out of money. A number of new investment products currently being developed allow for investors to systematically draw down their capital in a very disciplined way.

## MYTH: RETIREES SHOULD TAKE LITTLE FINANCIAL RISK

It is a widely held belief that retired investors should dramatically reduce the risk in their investment portfolio by selling off their stocks and purchasing low risk/income-producing securities.

REALITY: This strategy might have been appropriate in the past, when people were expected to live only a few years after they retired. Today, many retirees can expect to live 25 to 30 years after retirement. Over a period this long, the short-term volatility, or risk, of equities will be smoothed out and their superior returns will help to protect capital against inflation. Over the long run, high inflation is a danger that can have a greater negative impact on the purchasing power of assets than the short-term risk of equities. The addition of some equity investments can reduce the overall risk of a portfolio containing 100 percent bonds.

## MYTH: RETIREES SHOULD MINIMIZE THEIR RRSP/RRIF WITHDRAWALS

Retirees are often led to believe that they should always minimize withdrawals from their RRSP(Registered Retirement Savings Plan) or RRIF (Registered Retirement Income Fund) in order to allow their investment income to compound tax-free.

REALITY: Retired investors in the top marginal tax bracket can always benefit from allowing their investment income to be deferred as long as possible. On the other hand, those in a relatively low tax bracket but with a relatively large RRSP can benefit from taking out more than the minimum in the early years of their retirement. By spreading the withdrawals out more evenly they can avoid the huge tax bills they may face in their 80s when they have to take out very large sums from their RRIFs at the highest marginal tax bracket. At that point they also risk having OAS (Old Age

Security) clawed back. Retirees generally spend more in the early years of their retirement. Taking the money out earlier also allows them to spend more on the things they want to do while they are still able to do them.

## MYTH: RETIREES DO NOT NEED ADVICE

Many investors enjoy the time they spend reading, researching, and managing their portfolios. When retired, they have more time to devote to this "hobby," and feel they can do it on their own, particularly with online access to investment information and online discount brokerage accounts, which make it easy and cheap to trade stocks.

REALITY: Although in theory everyone can manage their investments effectively, the sad fact is that most people do not. Managing investments is not about buying and selling stocks; it is about following a plan and understanding and managing risk. These are concepts professional money managers understand but many do-it-yourselfers fail to grasp. The large quantity of information available does not make investing any easier; in many ways it makes it more difficult, because more time is spent wading through the random noise of the markets to find the truly valuable piece of information. People acting on their own will show great interest in the stocks they own as they are rising. However, in poor markets, many cannot bear to look at their portfolios and often ignore them, only to see many of their gains wiped out. Emotions often get in the way of sound judgment. When you are young you can afford to make foolish mistakes, but when you are retired those same mistakes can have more serious consequences.

For most retirees, some good advice is helpful. The key to success is getting advice that is free from the conflict of interest that usually exists when financial advisors are paid based on what they sell rather than on the quality of their advice.

## MYTH: THE MOST IMPORTANT OBJECTIVE IN RETIREMENT IS TO MAINTAIN YOUR PRE-RETIREMENT STANDARD OF LIVING

This myth implies that the higher your standard of living, the more content you will be. The myth is perpetuated by a financial services industry that has much to gain by equating more wealth with greater happiness. According to this way of thinking, the more you save, the more your wealth grows, the more you make, the happier you become—and the more you invest in their products.

REALITY: The most important objective in retirement is to maximize your quality of life, not your standard of living. Having financial security and a comfortable standard of living will certainly add to your quality of life. However, research has shown that after your basic needs are met, many other things, such as good health, a good relationship, family and friends, and having a purpose in life that makes you look forward to getting up every day are more important than a higher standard of living.

## What you can do now
- Keep an open mind to the possibilities that retirement offers.
- Base decisions on your own goals and personal circumstances.
- Ignore the stereotypes.
- Question the assumptions about retirement.
- Think of retirement as your new career.

## The bottom line
Many misconceptions about retirement are based on generalizations that do not take into account the diverse group of current and future retirees and the unique circumstances of each individual. Blindly following some of these preconceived notions about retirement can take you down the wrong path and limit your options and choices for the future. Retirement today is not like it was 20 or 30 years ago. Although some recent retirees will have a "traditional" retirement, the number of people who choose this course will be smaller in the future.

# Rule 2
## Plan Today for Tomorrow's Retirement

We like to divide the retirement planning exercise into two different parts: the planning that takes place years before you actually think about retiring and the planning that takes place in the five or so years before you retire. Twenty or 30 years prior to retirement, planning is all about saving money or building wealth to finance your retirement. In the few years before retiring, the focus shifts to lifestyle issues such as when to quit work and where to live and what to do when you stop working. Because these lifestyle issues all have financial consequences, lifestyle planning and financial planning are not separate exercises; instead, together they form the basis for the overall planning and preparation process.

As a future retiree, you face issues and choices surrounding retirement that are more complex than those faced by past generations. To understand your choices and to ensure that you make the correct decisions, you will need to take the time to plan and prepare carefully. Here are some of the reasons why.

### OPTIONS OVERLOAD
As an individual approaching retirement, you now have more options than ever before. Will you pursue an active lifestyle involving sports and travel, or a less active one of volunteer work or maybe going back to school? Will you stay in the same community with friends and family or move to a location that better suits your desired lifestyle? When it's time to give up your present job, will you work part-time, start a new career, or quit cold turkey? The financial options available for investing and managing your money are extensive and require careful consideration in themselves.

### INCREASED LONGEVITY
With the increase in life expectancy it will not be uncommon for people to be living in retirement for over 30 years. The longer your life expectancy, the greater the need to make long-range plans to ensure your capital will last into old age. An increase in longevity means that several generations of the same family will be alive at the same time, making planning an

overall family exercise as opposed to an exercise for just one person or a couple. It is also likely that some seniors will have to support both parents and children simultaneously.

## INCREASED SELF-RELIANCE

More and more often, retirees are going to have to rely on their own resources to fund their retirement. The traditional company pension plan, which provided a guaranteed monthly pension for life, is becoming a less common option. Government entitlement programs, although an essential retirement resource for most retirees, are usually not sufficient. It follows that the more you have to rely on yourself, the greater the need to be properly prepared for retirement in order to minimize costly mistakes.

## DIFFICULTY SAVING FOR RETIREMENT

Don't worry. We are not going to lecture you on why you need to save for your retirement. Banks, insurance companies, and mutual fund companies, through their advertising, do that already. Saving money is not a virtue. It is an economic choice. Saving money is the decision to defer current consumption (spending your money today) in order to have the money for future consumption (spending your money tomorrow). It is a difficult balancing act for most people.

A study done by the Consumer Federation of America and Wachovia in 2007 found that 17 percent of Americans said they could not afford to save at all, while 35 percent said that they were not saving enough to meet short- or long-term financial needs. For those who were not saving adequately, the reasons cited for not doing so (respondents could choose as many reasons as they wanted) were large regular expenses (72 percent), unexpected expenses (72 percent), and low or unreliable earnings (66 percent). Other factors cited as barriers included credit card debt (42 percent), impulse spending (37 percent), spending to feel good (29 percent), and social pressure from family and friends (20 percent). Economic as well as social and psychological factors were mentioned as barriers to saving. The problem is not simply a lack of will power or self-discipline.

In the paper "Motivating Retirement Planning: Problems and Solutions," Gary Selnow discusses the difficulties of motivating people to save. He says,

"Investing for retirement is different from just about anything else people are asked to do. Along nearly every dimension, tucking away money for a more secure tomorrow violates basic human inclinations. The savings ethic is resistant to nearly all motivators we commonly use to encourage desired behaviours . . ." Some of the reasons for this resistance include:

- The reality of paying the bills for today, when the needs are the greatest, will generally win out over the daydream of a pleasant and financially secure retirement.
- Money spent today can provide instant gratification, whereas money saved defers it.
- Savings set aside for retirement provide no current satisfaction. They provide only a promise in an uncertain future.
- There will be no penalty or dire consequences today if people fail to put aside money for tomorrow.
- People believe they can avoid saving today because they will have lots of time to save for tomorrow.

Most people are "hardwired" to spend. Although the brain knows that saving money is the "right thing," our short-term inclination is towards instant gratification. Overcoming this natural tendency is the challenge that you face when saving for retirement. In the study mentioned earlier, the people who did save identified their most effective strategies. The most important ones they mentioned were avoiding credit card debt, planning and monitoring of spending, and making regular contributions to workplace retirement plans.

So what's the good news? Research suggests there are two ways to motivate people and help them save more—financial education and planning. Workers who attend company-sponsored financial education programs tend to have higher participation rates and contribution rates in saving plans than workers whose employers do not offer such programs. Also, individuals who engage in financial planning tend to have a higher net worth at retirement.

The goal of the authors of the published research paper "Baby Boomer Retirement Security: The Roles of Planning, Financial Literacy, and

Housing Wealth," was "to evaluate how successful individuals plan for retirement, whether financial literacy is associated with better planning, and whether retirement preparedness is associated with those behaviors." The study found that those who planned even a little were much better off in retirement than those who didn't plan at all. Furthermore, the study found that financial literacy was very important in determining whether or not people planned. The financially illiterate tended not to plan, while the financially literate did. Planners save more and end up with greater wealth at retirement.

People are more likely to reach their goals and translate intentions into actions when they have developed a plan. If, like many people, you do not have the self-discipline to save, you will find that financial planning can help you control your spending. Even the simplest planning activity, such as writing down the steps to implement a task, can increase the likelihood that you will follow through.

## REDUCE YOUR ANXIETY SURROUNDING RETIREMENT

As people approach their retirement date, they have many concerns: about their finances, about filling up the time in the day, and about their future health. Concern is a normal response as we come to grips with an uncertain future. At all major milestones in our lives, the anticipation of the event is often mixed with feelings of anxiety. Retirement is no different, and for some people making the transition from a working to a nonworking life is a very stressful time.

Financial concerns are often the most troubling and are frequently reinforced by the messages we receive through the marketing and advertising programs of our major financial institutions. But, in fact, we do not have financial concerns only at the point of retirement; we worry about money throughout our lives. Will I have enough money to buy my first home and make the monthly mortgage payments? How will I ever pay off all those student loans? Can I afford to leave my job and stay home and raise our child? Will my business ever start to make money? However, once you are actually retired, financial concerns often become much less serious. In the Canadian Community Health survey of 2002, only about 5 percent of those over the age of 65 felt that their financial situation contributed to feelings of stress. This rate was lower than that of any other age group. About 30 percent of seniors said that the biggest source of stress in their lives was their own health, followed by the health of family members.

The EBRI (Employee Benefit Research Institute), a U.S.-based non-profit, non-partisan organization, conducts an annual Retirement Confidence Survey. One thousand workers and 252 retirees were interviewed for the 2006 survey. When asked "How confident are you in having enough money to live comfortably throughout your retirement years?" only 24 percent of the workers were "very confident," compared to 40 percent of the retirees. Thirty-five percent of the workers were "very confident in having enough money to take care of basic expenses in retirement," compared to 44 percent of those already retired. When asked "How confident were you of doing a good job of preparing financially for retirement?" again only 25 percent of workers were "very confident," versus 42 percent of retirees. The same trend was evident when the interviewers asked about paying for medical expenses or long-term care—a greater percentage of retirees were "very confident," compared to people who were still working.

Similar research studies show the same results. Those participants who were already retired were generally more confident and less concerned about their financial future than those on the cusp of retiring. Why? First, there is the fear of the unknown. Retirees have first-hand experience about living in retirement. Having greater familiarity and understanding of the issues reduces their concerns. Second, some retirees face their concerns head-on and change their financial behaviour. If they are concerned about running out of money, they cut back on their spending. If they believe inflation is a big issue, they make changes to their investment strategy.

## What you can do now

- Start talking to your spouse about retirement.
- Take responsibility for your own future.
- Use your concerns as a source of motivation.
- Arm yourself with the right information.
- Examine your options and analyze the trade-offs you might have to make.
- Don't procrastinate—start the process right away.

## The bottom line

It is quite common to suffer from anxiety over your finances as retirement approaches. Those who are anxious will overestimate the risks and underestimate their resources. There are three choices you can make. You can ignore your concerns and hope that the anxiety will go away. You can continue to worry and do nothing about it. Or you can face your concerns head-on. Proper planning and preparation will lower your anxiety and increase your confidence in dealing with the uncertain future that lies ahead.

# Part 2

## Think about the Retirement Plan that's Right for You

WE ALL HAVE A LOTTERY FANTASY. WHEN WE BUY A TICKET OR SEE THAT THE FIRST PRIZE OF THE Super 7 or the Lotto 6/49 is $5 million, we indulge in a few minutes of pure fantasy. In an instant we plan how we would spend the money. We dream about buying a new house or taking a big trip. We imagine the happiness on our children's faces when we give them each a million dollars. And we see ourselves quitting our jobs and maybe even telling our boss exactly what we think of him.

As we approach retirement, most of us also have a retirement fantasy. It could be moving to a sun-drenched island in the Caribbean, or building a dream house, or going on exotic vacations. It might be as simple as sleeping in every morning or spending more time with family and friends. Although only a lucky few ever win the lottery, almost everyone will eventually retire and have the chance to turn their retirement fantasy into reality. The question now is whether your retirement will be analogous to winning the $5 million or the $10 consolation prize.

Creating a vision for your future is one of the first and most important steps you can take to ensure a successful retirement. Initially the vision might be very vague, such as living in a warm climate, spending more time playing golf or taking a course or two at university. As you approach retirement and start forming more concrete goals, your vision will become clearer. Now is the time to move from the fantasy vision to goals that are realistic and achievable.

In creating our vision, there are two natural tendencies that most of us have to overcome. The first is to become fixated on the first couple of years of retirement. The reality is that your retirement might last over 30 years. Decisions that make sense for the short term might be detrimental over the long term. The second tendency is to fail to recognize how much you will change as you age. We tend to think that we will have the same attitudes, concerns, needs, and desires that we have today. We also often overlook how the aging process will affect us mentally and physically.

# Rule 3

## Understand that a Successful Retirement Requires More than Money

To start preparing for your next phase in life, ask yourself a simple question. What makes me happy? Planning for retirement is not just about financial security; it is about planning for a happy and fulfilling life.

Wealth can buy a higher standard of living and the peace of mind that comes with financial security. But does more money equal more happiness? According to a 2006 Statistics Canada study, the median net wealth in Canada for people 65 and over was $157,000. Are those who fall into the bottom 50 percent going to be automatically less happy or less content in retirement than those in the top 50 percent? Of course not. Here's why.

### WHAT MAKES PEOPLE HAPPY IN RETIREMENT?

In "What Makes Retirees Happy," a 2005 study sponsored by the Center for Retirement Research at Boston College, Keith Bender and Natalia Jivan reported that about 60 percent of retirees surveyed were very satisfied with their life, about 30 percent were moderately satisfied and only about 8 percent were not at all satisfied. Over 50 percent found retirement better, about 30 percent found it about the same, and only 17 percent felt it was worse than life before retirement. In general, most people found life in retirement satisfying and as good as, or better than, life pre-retirement.

In their study, Bender and Jivan did find that as wealth and income rose, the probability of being happy improved, results that have been shown in other studies. However, the effects of wealth were a minor factor in explaining satisfaction in retirement. Other factors were far more significant.

For example, those who had defined benefits pension plans had a better chance of being happy than those who had defined contributions plans or no pension at all. Having a guaranteed income provided by a defined benefits plan led to greater satisfaction. Those who had both a defined benefits plan and a defined contributions plan had an even higher probability of being happy than those with just one plan. Having one plan that provided steady income and another plan tied to overall market performance (a plan that the retirees could control) helped them feel more secure.

According to Bender and Jivan, two factors stand out as particularly important in determining well-being—health and the reason for retirement. In the study, those who were in poor health experienced a dramatically lower level of well-being. They were 19.7 percent more likely to be dissatisfied with their retirement than those who were in good or excellent health.

The fact that health is a major factor in determining well-being in retirement should come as no surprise. What might come as a surprise is that, according to the study, the most important determinant of satisfaction was whether the decision to retire was voluntary or involuntary. People who had been forced out of work due to ill health, poor performance, or company restructuring were less likely to be satisfied than those who had retired voluntarily. These people were often both psychologically and financially unprepared for retirement.

In Canada, the findings of a similar study that used data from the 2002 General Social Survey were published in the autumn 2005 edition of *Canadian Social Trends*. In their article "What Makes Retirement Enjoyable," Grant Schellenberg, Martin Turcotte, and Bali Ram reported that marital status, or more precisely, a change in marital status, was also an important factor in determining well-being. Of those who were not married before retirement and then married, 68 percent reported enjoying life more than before retirement. Some people who divorced or separated after retirement enjoyed life less (10 percent), but the majority (60 percent) reported enjoying life more. Not surprisingly, those who had lost a spouse after retiring experienced a decline in happiness.

This study also showed that the enjoyment wealth or income add to retirement is marginal. Of retirees with household incomes greater than $60,000, 52 percent reported greater enjoyment after retirement, versus the average of 47 percent. However, a change in a person's financial situation after retirement had significant repercussions. Those whose financial situation improved after retirement were more likely to show an increase in enjoyment (64 percent) versus those whose finances had deteriorated (39 percent). This would suggest that how well you manage your money may be more important in determining satisfaction in retirement than the actual amount you have when you first retire.

The age at which people retired proved to be an important factor in their enjoyment as well. Those who were 50 to 54 when they retired had a 59 percent probability of satisfaction, versus 40 percent of those who retired at age 65 to 74. It could be that those who retired early may have been eager to do so and thus planned to make the most of retired life. In fact, a very interesting part of the study was whether participants had prepared for retirement. They were asked if they had gathered information about retirement, developed new hobbies, become involved in volunteer work, or participated in physical activities. Those who had engaged in three or four of these preparations were more likely to report increased enjoyment (59 percent) than those who engaged in none (43 percent). Preparing for this new stage of life does seem to improve enjoyment. The better prepared you are, the more likely it is that retirement will meet your expectations.

## CAN YOU BE HAPPY IF YOUR STANDARD OF LIVING DROPS?

Many workers ready to retire are concerned that they might not be able to maintain the same standard of living. In a Harris Interactive survey that asked retirees to compare their standard of living pre-retirement and post-retirement, 41 percent found that their standard of living was lower in retirement and only 16 percent found that it was higher. Yet when the same group was asked to compare their level of happiness before and after retirement, 53 percent were in fact happier after and only 21 percent were less happy. Even though many people's standard of living suffered, they were in fact happier in retirement. Retirement living for most people is an enjoyable part of their lives. It is so enjoyable that people retire early, even though this causes a drop in their standard of living.

## CHECKLIST FOR A SATISFYING AND SUCCESSFUL RETIREMENT

HEALTH: When we are young, we take our health for granted. But as we age, we can no longer assume we will always live in good health. Take the necessary steps to maintain your health. Regular physical activity adds to your well-being over and above the health benefits it provides. (See Section 4.)

**WEALTH:** What is important is not your absolute level of wealth but your relative level. People who have more money than others of the same age group will in general be happier. Similarly, trying to keep up with the Joneses makes people unhappy. Even affluent people are more likely to be unhappy when they live in a neighbourhood where others are better off than they are. What is important is to live within your means and, if necessary, to lower your expectations to ensure that you have the means to support your lifestyle. The gap between the money you have and the money you need is more important than your absolute level of wealth. Having the security of a steady income that is not affected by the fluctuations of the stock market will also add to your contentment.

**MEANINGFUL ACTIVITIES:** It is important to engage in activities that provide life with a sense of meaning and purpose—in other words, spending time doing things you find challenging and valuable. This could be hobbies, full- or part-time work, or volunteer duties. Working in retirement often improves the level of life satisfaction beyond the extra income it might provide.

**PREPARATION AND PLANNING:** The better prepared you are, both financially and psychologically, the better your retirement will be. People who can control when and how they retire will generally be happier than those who are forced into this stage of life. Before you actually retire, get involved in activities you plan to do when you reach that stage. When you analyze your options and make sensible choices you will have a more contented and enjoyable experience. Careful planning and preparation will also allow you to have realistic expectations of the life that lies ahead and will ensure that you meet your goals. People who have written financial plans are generally more confident and optimistic about their retirement than those who have not.

**RELATIONSHIPS:** Having a good marriage and a good relationship with your extended family and close friends is important throughout your life but it is even more important in retirement. Seeing friends regularly helps improve mental health and general well-being.

**HAPPINESS:** Recent research suggests people who are happy tend to be more successful than those who are not. This is quite contrary to the theory that success makes people happy. Happy people tend to be more confident, optimistic, and energetic and more likely to work towards new goals. Being happy and having a positive attitude will help you achieve a successful retirement.

## What you can do now

- Remember the times in your life when you were the happiest and most content.
- Determine which parts of your job provide you with the most satisfaction.
- Understand how you enjoy spending your time.
- Before retirement, get involved in activities you plan to do once you stop working.
- Ask people who are retired what they enjoy about it.
- Don't wait for retirement to enjoy life—start today.

## The bottom line

Retirement living for most people is an enjoyable part of life. It is so enjoyable that people will retire early, even though this causes a drop in their standard of living compared to what they would enjoy if they continued to work. When planning for retirement, it is important to remember it is not just about the money. It is about having a happy, satisfying, and contented life. The people who are most likely to achieve these goals are the same ones who planned for them.

# Rule 4

## Don't Forget the Impact of Aging on Your Health

Our health is something that most of us take for granted, except of course on those occasions when we become sick. At these times, relieving pain and discomfort becomes the number one priority. In the years leading up to retirement, you can no longer take your health for granted. An enjoyable retirement is largely dependent on good health.

Besides the obvious quality of life considerations it entails, your health has important financial implications. One of the main reasons that people are forced to retire early, even before they can afford it, is due to poor health. It is also one of the primary reasons seniors sell their family home. Spending generally decreases as people age, but health-care costs go up. Seniors who are in poor health spend more on drugs, home care, and nursing homes. On the other hand, the healthier you are, the longer you are likely to live, and the longer your financial resources have to last. Understanding how your health will change over time will ensure you are better prepared for retirement, both emotionally and financially.

### OLD AGE CAN BE A TIME OF GOOD HEALTH, BOTH MENTAL AND PHYSICAL

Our bodies change as we age. Thinning hair, sagging skin, slowing response times, decline in hearing and vision are all signs of the natural aging process. As we get older, blood pressure, cholesterol levels, body weight, and blood sugar levels tend to increase and bone density and the immune function tend to decline, resulting in an increased risk of disease. Inevitably, aging will result in the onset of illness and death, but this does not have to take place until many years into retirement. It is possible, with wise lifestyle choices, to live a relatively healthy life into your 80s and 90s. Even those with chronic conditions can, with medication and proper care, maintain their independence and live relatively healthy and pain-free lives.

We used to believe that getting old meant getting sick and that once we were sick a return to good health was impossible. Fortunately, we have learned that we can take steps to reverse years of abuse and neglect. Older people who start doing aerobic exercise can boost cardiovascular fitness by the same average 10 to 30 percent as younger people. Those who have started muscle-building workouts in their 80s and 90s have doubled or tripled their strength in a matter of months.

A study of men over the age of 60 found that those who worked themselves into shape during a five-year period had half the cardiovascular and death rates of those who remained unfit. Weight loss and appropriate exercise can reduce arthritis pain. Experts report that exercise can reverse about half of the physical decline that is normally attributed to aging. Moreover, regular exercise can improve older people's mental agility. Research suggests that exercise boosts the production of certain brain chemicals that promote the growth of new cells.

Studies of twins showed that only one third of the loss of physical function related to aging could be blamed on heredity; the larger part stemmed mainly from poor health habits. Taking steps to manage lifestyle choices, including getting proper nutrition and exercise, can slow, stop, or even reverse the changes once blamed on aging.

In addition, medical interventions such as hearing aids and low-vision devices, heart and diabetes drugs, and surgery for arthritis and cataracts can fend off disability and in some cases prolong life. Researchers estimate that if people born today lead healthy lifestyles, their average lifespan could soar from the current 80 years to 100 years.

Similarly, it is not aging that leads to intellectual decline but rather a lifestyle that lacks stimulation. Much of mental slowdown appears to be preventable or reversible. Mental exercise, like physical exercise, may also help preserve cognitive ability. Training older people in various mental skills can reverse up to two decades of memory loss. Doing anything that is mentally challenging, such as practising a musical instrument, playing chess, or doing crossword puzzles can help maintain and possibly even help restore mental functioning.

## SENIORS AND GOOD HEALTH

A study carried out jointly by Statistics Canada and the Canadian Institute for Health Information examined a range of health care issues confronting seniors. The findings, published in 2006 in a report titled "Health at Older Ages," provides valuable insight into the future health care needs of all those who are planning for retirement.

According to the World Health Organization, "good health is not merely the absence of illness or infirmity, but a state of complete physical, mental and social well-being." For the purposes of the study just referred to, people were considered to be in good health if they met four main criteria: good functional health, independence in activities of daily living, positive self-perceived general health, and positive self-perceived mental health.

In Canada, the percentage of people in good health was fairly constant at about 81 percent until the age of 44, when it began to decline. Sixty-five percent of those age 65 to 74 were in good health, 45 percent of those age 75 to 84, and only 22 percent of those 85 and older. The good news is that seniors' self-perceived general health does not deteriorate as rapidly as functional health, which is defined as the lack of disabilities.

TABLE 2.1
PERCENTAGE OF PEOPLE IN GOOD HEALTH

|  | age 65–74 | age 75–84 | age 85+ |
|---|---|---|---|
| Good functional health | 80 | 64 | 37 |
| Independent in activities of daily living | 88 | 70 | 41 |
| Good self-perceived mental health | 95 | 93 | 95 |
| Good self-perceived general health | 79 | 68 | 63 |
| Overall good health | 65 | 45 | 22 |

Source: Statistics Canada, "Health at Older Ages"

As Table 2.1 shows, 80 percent of seniors age 65 to 74 still have good functional health. Within this age range, 88 percent of people are able to live independently, doing day-to-day chores without any outside assistance. Although this number drops to 41 percent for seniors older than 85, it is still a larger percentage than one might expect. Self-perceived mental health does not appear to change at all with age. About 95 percent of seniors over 65 perceive themselves to have good mental health.

The difference between functional health and self-perceived general health suggests that as people get older they compare their health to that of others in their own age group, not to the health of younger individuals or to their own health at a younger age. Since many of the friends of men and women in their 80s and 90s might have died or become very ill,

## Still Active at 93

My father moved into a retirement home a couple of years ago at 91, when he felt he was too old to live on his own. He was born and raised on a farm, served in the Second World War, and worked hard all his life, as did most of his generation. He worked full-time until he was 70 and then part time until he was 75. When he was 65, he took a couple of years off to look after my sick mother until she died.

Although he has slowed down a bit, Dad is still in remarkably good health at 93. He has a bit of arthritis, he just successfully underwent some cataract surgeries on his eyes, and he takes medication for his blood pressure. He still goes on his regular walks, twice a day, rain or shine, summer or winter. He plays bridge and cribbage with the "girls" in the home and wins his share of Scrabble games with me even though he completed only high school and I spent six years at university.

He leads a contented, simple, low-stress life, eats small but well-balanced meals, drinks the occasional glass of wine, gets regular exercise, has a sense of community, and keeps his mind mentally stimulated. In short, his good health at the age of 93 is a testament to a simple but healthy lifestyle.

K.H., age 57

those seniors surviving would consider themselves to be in good health. Although seniors' functional health might be declining, many still feel positive about their general level of health.

A significant finding of the study was the strong relationship between good health and behavioural and psychosocial factors. The study lists behavioural factors as leisure-time physical activity, alcohol use, body mass index (BMI), daily fruit and vegetable consumption, and smoking status. Psychosocial factors are life stress and sense of community belonging.

Regular physical activity is the most important thing that seniors can do to maintain health and mobility. According to the study, of those who were physically active more than three times a week, 67 percent were in good health, versus 36 percent of those who were active less than once a week. Those seniors who occasionally drank alcohol were generally in better health than either those who were heavy drinkers or those who abstained from alcohol altogether. Seniors who had a normal weight or were slightly overweight were generally in better health than those who were either underweight or obese. Not surprisingly, nutrition was very important, with 62 percent of those who ate five or more servings of fruits and vegetables a day considered to be in good health, versus 52 percent of those who ate less than three servings.

Low stress and a strong sense of community belonging were also key predictors of good health. Seniors who reported low stress in their lives were almost twice as likely to be in good health (62 percent) as those who had high stress levels (32 percent). Sixty-two percent of seniors who had a strong connection to the community were healthy versus only 49 percent of those whose sense of community was weak. Social relationships and affiliations were also found to be very positive factors in maintaining mental and physical health.

According to the study, the higher the total number of positive behavioural and psychosocial factors in a person's life, the greater the probability of good health. For people over the age of 65, the probability of good health was only 18 percent if one or no factors were present. This figure rose to 56 percent if four factors were present and to 81 percent if all seven factors were present—the same probability of good health as that enjoyed by people age 18 to 44. In other words, it is possible for many seniors to maintain the health that they enjoyed at an earlier age if they live a healthy lifestyle.

## LIVING INDEPENDENTLY INTO OLD AGE

Like most people who are planning for their later years, you may dread the thought of being forced to live in an institutional setting, tucked away in the corner of some nursing home, forgotten and neglected by friends and family. What are your chances of ending up in a long-term care facility? Surprisingly low.

The "Health at Older Ages" study also examined two different measures of dependence, Activities of Daily Living (ADLs) and Instrumental Activities of Daily Living (IADLs). ADLs are the tasks considered vital to retaining personal independence, such as bathing, dressing, eating, taking medication, and moving around the house. IADLs include preparing meals, doing everyday housework, getting to appointments, grocery shopping, banking, and paying bills. Almost everyone who is ADL-dependent is also IADL-dependent.

The report found that overall, very few seniors were ADL-dependent. Only about 6 percent of males and 7 percent of females between 65 and 84 fell into this category. These rates increased dramatically to over 20 percent for those 85 and older. People who are ADL-dependent might have to move to an assisted care facility if their spouse or primary caregiver dies. But, as you can see, 80 percent of men and women in the study that were over the age of 85 were still able to lead relatively independent lives in their own homes.

For seniors betweeen 65 and 74, 15 percent of males and 29 percent of females might require some assistance with day-to-day activities. For those over the age of 85, the percentages were considerably higher, with 48 percent of males and 65 percent of females requiring some assistance.

At every age group, women are more likely than men to be dependent on others for daily chores. Seniors who are IADL-independent typically live in their own homes and receive help with their daily activities from a spouse, family member, friend, neighbour, or community health services worker.

## What you can do now

- Get regular checkups from your doctor.
- Take the necessary steps to keep in good health.
- Become more physically active.
- If you have a workplace health plan, understand what your benefits will be before and during retirement.
- Determine if it makes sense to have elective surgery or major dental work while still employed.

## The bottom line

Good health is a wonderful gift that allows us to do those things that we enjoy. Poor health is a liability that limits what we can do and leads to greater financial expenses. We cannot stop the aging process, but we can understand it and become better prepared for it.

# Rule 5

## Realize that There Are Many Roads Leading to Retirement

Although it seems like a contradiction, work is a viable option for many people during their retirement. Some retirees work out of financial necessity and others do it for fun. According to Statistics Canada, as of 2004, 21.8 percent of men between the ages of 65 and 69 and 6.9 percent of those over the age of 70 were still working. Moreover, as many recent surveys suggest, the number of working retirees is expected to increase in the future. Will you be one of them?

When to stop working is one of the most fundamental decisions you will have to make. With the end of mandatory retirement across Canada, employees can work as long as they want—assuming that they remain healthy or are not forced out due to restructuring or poor performance.

Many individuals enjoy their work for other reasons than the pay they receive. They look forward each day to the mental challenges of the job, the social network it provides, the structure it adds to their life, or the prestige the position offers. For these people, retiring might be a mistake that will affect not only their financial security but also their quality of life. If they cannot replace the positive aspects of the job with meaningful activities in their retirement, then this phase can be a time of regret. Continuing to work makes sense because it allows people to maintain or improve their standard of living, as well as carry on doing things they enjoy.

For other people, the situation is the opposite. They cannot wait to retire. They might be bored or find their work physically or mentally draining and stressful. Some might have already retired—on the job. Even though they show up to work, they are not committed to it and have mentally checked out. Many boomers have activities and hobbies that they would like to pursue but do not have the time for while they're working. For these people, the decision to retire is an easy one to make—they will retire as soon as they can afford to. The only difficulty is saving enough money to ensure they will have the necessary financial security.

## MAKING THE TRANSITION INTO RETIREMENT

Many recent studies confirm that people would like to work in retirement. *The Globe and Mail* reported that only 13 percent of baby boomers surveyed did not want to work at all, compared to 59 percent who wanted to work part-time and 25 percent who wanted to do volunteer work. A Merrill Lynch study in the United States found that people on average wanted to retire at age 61 but to stop working entirely at age 70. However, those who wanted to work in retirement often wanted to do something completely different from the "same old" job. Of those age 41 to 59 who wanted to work, 65 percent were interested in pursuing a different line of work, versus only 35 percent who wanted to continue in the same one. Moreover, many had taken steps to prepare for another job by researching specific opportunities, talking to people about it, and attending classes or training sessions.

The desire to work after retiring from a principal job has spawned a number of new buzzwords. Professionals and executives are "re-careering," changing professions in mid-to-late stages of their career. Many are pursuing consulting opportunities or starting a new business. Others are "downshifting" to a less stressful or part-time job. Rather than climbing up the corporate ladder, they are choosing to climb down. Some workers are "job sharing," where a regular, full-time job is shared by two people, each working part-time. Other people are taking "phased retirement," gradually working fewer hours or taking on different roles in the company until they retire. For those who find retirement less than satisfying, there is always "return-ment," or coming out of retirement to go back to work.

Increasingly, the lines between working and retirement are blurring for people in their 50s, 60s, and even 70s. The dramatic change between the working and the retirement years is morphing into a more gradual progression from work to leisure or cycling back and forth between the two. Why? Today's older people are healthier and more involved in the knowledge economy. They do not have the same physically demanding jobs that people did a generation or two ago. Also, today fewer workers are eligible for traditional defined benefits pension plans, and more and more people might have to work in their retirement out of necessity rather than choice.

As many studies have found, work can have many beneficial effects. It can increase people's sense of well-being and be an important source of friends. Older people who are employed in low-stress jobs with the schedule they desire experience increased health. Physically demanding jobs have also been shown to have a positive effect on the health of people 65 and older.

Wanting to work in retirement is one thing; another is finding employment doing something that pays well and is meaningful. As baby boomers start retiring, companies will begin to experience labour shortages. Employers will have to be creative to retain and attract staff and one way of doing this is to target older workers. In an effort to maintain their workforce, many firms are expected to abolish early retirement incentives and replace them with incentives to work longer. To keep older workers on staff, companies may have to offer flexible work schedules and more options for part-time jobs. They may have to aggressively recruit older workers and make their company more attractive to them. In the end, workers will have more, not fewer, options as they transition into retirement.

A 2006 study sponsored by the Vanguard Center for Retirement Research and Harris Interactive examined how people make the transition from work to retirement. Based on the work histories of Americans age 55 to 69, the study found that six different patterns have emerged. The study calls these patterns: Early Retirees, Work and Play, Still Working, Returnees, Spouse's Retirement, and Never Retire.

EARLY RETIREES: Individuals on this path (29 percent of Americans age 55 to 69) exit the full-time workforce mostly in their 50s and stop all work thereafter. Typically these people have good savings, excellent financial habits, and a pension plan. However, also likely to be on this path are people in poor health and those with a high school education or less.

WORK AND PLAY: Fewer in number than the early retirees (12 percent), many of these people leave full-time work in their 50s but then quickly take on part-time work or become self-employed. They are likely to have a pension plan. The decision of these semi-retired people to work is motivated by the desire to be more active and have more discretionary spending, as well as by their enjoyment of their job.

**STILL WORKING:** People in this group leave the workforce later than those in the two previous paths, mostly in their 60s. They represent 35 percent of all retirees. Even after they retire from their full-time jobs, most continue to engage in part-time work or are self-employed in their late 60s. Typically they have a lower level of financial resources than those on the previous two paths and are unlikely to have a company pension plan. These individuals are likely to be healthy, female, and have an associate's, bachelor's, or graduate-school degree. They also are more likely to include the divorced, widowed, or separated.

**RETURNEES:** Those individuals who decided to return to work after retiring represent 5 percent of retirees. They leave work quite early, typically in their 50s, and stop working completely—then return a few years later. They are likely to be male or covered by a pension plan, but they also are likely not to have saved much in the past, or to be divorced, widowed, or separated. For these people, emotional and financial factors are both important drivers for returning to work. In many ways retiring early was a mistake for them.

**SPOUSE'S RETIREMENT:** This group (9 percent of those age 55 to 69) includes individuals with a much lower participation in full-time work in their 40s and 50s than average. They are most likely to be married women in excellent health who retired when their spouses did.

**NEVER RETIRE:** This group (10 percent of those age 55 to 69) continues to work in their 60s. They intend never to retire, although they plan to shift from full-time to part-time work in their mid-to-late 60s. They are generally in excellent health, motivated by both a desire to be active and a need to meet their basic living expenses.

In the three groups where work plays a major role in retirement—Work and Play, Returnees, and Never Retire—the principal reason for continuing to work is the value people place on it. Financial reasons are important as well. Many people who plan never to retire work out of necessity. Obviously, each individual's path to retirement is defined by his or her relationship to work. Choosing the right path can make the difference between a successful and an unsuccessful retirement.

### TABLE 2.2
#### MOTIVATIONS FOR CONTINUING TO WORK—INDIVIDUALS AGE 55-69

| Motivation | Work & Play (%) | Returnees (%) | Never Retire (%) |
|---|---|---|---|
| Like being active | 66 | 58 | 71 |
| Like work I'm doing | 55 | 56 | 69 |
| Like social interaction | 37 | 39 | 43 |
| Want extra money | 62 | 53 | 41 |
| Need to meet basic expenses | 32 | 52 | 58 |

Source: Vanguard Center for Retirement Research, "Six Paths to Retirement," 2007

## DOWNSHIFTING INTO RETIREMENT

Some people decide to work fewer hours or shift to a simpler or less stressful job in the years leading up to retirement. "Downshifting" essentially involves a change in a person's relationship to work. A job, and the income earned from it, is no longer the primary focus of their life. For many people, downshifting is the first transition in moving from a life of work to a life of leisure.

### TABLE 2.3
#### ACTUAL AND EXPECTED DOWNSHIFTING

| Ages | Have downshifted (%) | Expect to downshift (%) |
|---|---|---|
| 40–44 | 0 | 76 |
| 45–49 | 0 | 75 |
| 50–54 | 17 | 58 |
| 55–59 | 19 | 53 |
| 60–64 | 29 | 36 |
| 65–69 | 21 | 35 |

Source: Vanguard Center for Retirement Research, "Six Paths to Retirement," 2007

According to the Vanguard Center study, downshifting is a significant trend. Of those age 55 to 69, 23 percent have already downshifted and

## Phasing into Golf

Steve was a lot older than all the other instructors at the golf school that I attended last winter, on the outskirts of Miami. Most of the instructors were in their 20s or early 30s, but Steve, who was in his 50s, was closer to my age.

Steve had always been passionate about golf—he was offered a university golf scholarship. Although he had a successful career at a major utility company in California, he started to grow tired of the endless commute and the long hours at the office. He knew he wanted to retire early, but if he stopped working in his early 50s he would not be able to retire in comfort. So Steve decided to become a golf instructor. He took all the required courses and even started to teach part-time at the local golf range. He arranged a buy-out with his employer, sold his house, and bought an RV.

He chose to work at a golf school that offered instruction at different golf courses throughout the United States. Rather than work in one location, he moved around the country as the seasons changed. He would teach in Florida in the winter, North Carolina in the spring, and Vermont in the summer. The next year he might teach at different locations. He had a wonderful nomadic life, working at something that he was passionate about.

another 43 percent expect to do so in the future. Of those who have already downshifted, 42 percent reduced the hours they work, 36 percent took a simpler job, and 22 percent did both. Only 34 percent of those who downshifted remained with their existing employer. Most people either went to a different employer (49 percent) or became self employed (17 percent). Of those who downshifted, 48 percent worked at a job that was the same or similar to their old one, while 52 percent took a job that was entirely different. People who plan to downshift in the future say they would like to remain with their current employer in the same line of work.

According to the study, the main reasons people chose to downshift were to take a less demanding job (40 percent), to have more free time (35 percent), or to retire from the old job (29 percent). Other reasons included health or disability problems (19 percent), dislike of the old job (14 percent), layoffs (11 percent), or caregiver duties.

Many individuals who are currently working would like to downshift to fewer hours of work or a less stressful job. Whether they will be able to do so is somewhat dependent on the willingness of employers to allow a flexible work arrangement. This is something that not all employers are willing to do. Some jobs are more suitable to downshifting than others. Teachers and professors might find it easy to reduce the number of hours they work by teaching fewer classes. Managers, on the other hand, would find it difficult to get the job done if they worked fewer hours.

It seems clear that, with an impending labour shortage as the baby boomers begin to retire, more companies will be willing to offer more flexible work arrangements for their current or potential employees. Companies that fail to do this may have problems retaining valuable human resources.

### What you can do now
- Determine when you want to retire from your job.
- Determine the path you want to take into retirement.
- Decide if you want to pursue a different job in retirement.
- Keep your current job skills up to date by taking advantage of any training opportunities your company has to offer.
- Take appropriate training if you desire a job in a different field.

- Discuss downshifting or phased-in retirement opportunities with your employer's HR department. Many of these opportunities are offered on a case-by-case basis.

## The bottom line

You need to consider the decision about when to retire, or whether to retire at all, carefully. Retirement nowadays involves more than just leisure activities. The trend in retirement today includes the option of work, either out of necessity or simply for personal satisfaction. Those who want to spend the final phase of their lives at a meaningful and well-paying job that offers the flexibility they desire should start planning for it five years before retirement.

# Rule 6

## Consider the Many Options for Your Future Housing Needs

The decision about where to live when you retire is almost as important as the decision about when to retire. The majority of retirees choose
to stay in their pre-retirement home; close ties to family, friends, and
community make this a natural choice. Others, however, decide to take
a chance and move to a dream location. This might mean moving to a
smaller, more "senior-friendly" community, a location that is closer to
their children and grandchildren, a part of the country with a milder climate, or even a different country. Many people rely on the equity in their
home to help finance their retirement, and the decision to downsize and
move to a less expensive community is as much a financial decision as it
is a lifestyle choice.

Many people have a strong emotional attachment to the home where
they lived and perhaps raised a family. It is a visible sign of their success
and hard work. For people in their 70s and 80s, living in their own home
is also a sign of their independence; it shows they are healthy enough to
look after themselves and maintain their home. For many people the family home is also their biggest financial asset.

The decision to move or stay put can have a major impact on financial security in retirement. For some, selling their home and moving can
simultaneously increase their financial security and their standard of living. For example, a couple living in an expensive large city, but with no ties
to it, can move to a smaller, less congested town. They can buy a house that
is better quality but costs less than their old one. If the new town offers
amenities the couple enjoys, the move can provide not only more money
in the bank and a better standard of living, but also a better quality of life.

Sooner or later, almost everyone will move from their pre-retirement
home. Some will downsize to a smaller house, condominium, or apartment. Others will move into a retirement home because they are no longer
able to look after themselves or their spouse. For most retirees, the real
issue is not if they will move from their home but when and how often
they will move from it.

# A Win, Win, Win Situation

Carol had lived in her home for 25 years. It was the house where she and her husband had raised their family and she continued to live there after he died five years ago. After retiring at the young age of 62 and living by herself, she was starting to feel more and more isolated. Many of her neighbourhood friends were moving away and were being replaced by young couples with small children. With neat lawns, mature trees, and excellent schools nearby, the neighbourhood was highly sought after by young families. But Carol's house was now a little rundown, in need of minor repairs and a major updating. And her beautiful gardens, which had once been her pride and joy, were now more of a chore to maintain than a pleasure. So finally, despite her emotional attachment to the house and her reluctance to disrupt her life, she decided to move.

Carol sold her home and bought a condo in a new 55+ development on the other side of town. Although her unit was smaller than her previous home, the rooms were bright and spacious, with an excellent floor plan. Besides, why did she need four bedrooms? Even including her monthly maintenance fees, the overall cost of running her new condo was still less than the cost of maintaining her previous home. Moreover, her unit would require minimal upkeep. With the $150,000 cash equity she had after selling her home, she treated herself to a sporty new car, replacing her 15-year-old tired sedan, and deposited the balance of the money in her investment account.

One of the things Carol did not anticipate was the number of new people she would meet, many similar to herself, empty nesters who had moved from their homes in the suburbs. She became quite close with a number of the ladies and even went on her first date since her husband died. Next year she is going on a trip to Italy with a friend from the complex and is learning Italian in preparation. She realizes that selling her home was the best decision she could have made; it gave her a new lease on life.

## WHY DO SENIORS MOVE?

By and large, as people age they tend to move less often, reflecting, among other things, lives that are more stable. A Canada Mortgage and Housing Corporation study found that in 2002 almost 50 percent of Canadian households had moved during the previous six years. While almost 100 percent of people under the age of 30 moved, this number dropped to 30 percent for those between the ages of 55 and 64, and to 20 percent for those over 65. In spite of having the freedom to move, older people are more reluctant to relocate because they generally develop strong attachments to their neighbourhood community. As well, the act of moving can be physically taxing, disruptive, and costly.

As one would expect, the reasons people moved varied depending on their age. For those under 55, a primary reason was the desire to live in a larger home. For people age 55 to 64, only 11.2 percent wanted a larger home and, after 65, the number dropped to below 5 percent. In fact, for 15.3 percent of those between the ages of 55 and 64, the primary reason to move was the desire to live in a smaller place. This figure rose to 20.4 percent for those age 65 to 74 and to 24 percent for those over 85.

More than 20 percent of those over age 65 listed family issues—divorce, children leaving home, death of a spouse, or moving in with family members—as the primary reason for moving. Deteriorating health was a negligible factor for moving for people under 65 but was the primary reason for those who were older (16.7 percent for those between 65 and 74, 33.1 percent for those between 75 and 84, and 42.3 percent for those over 85).

In planning and preparing for retirement, one of the most important decisions is where to live. For older seniors, health and family issues are the main considerations in determining whether to stay or move. It is better to anticipate the changes in your housing requirements so that you have control over when and where you move, if moving is necessary.

## RETIREMENT LIVING TRENDS

The housing market for seniors and retirees will explode as the baby boomers begin to retire. Businesses are well aware of this demographic trend and have plans to capitalize on the potential growth opportunities.

For example, Royal LePage has created a Seniors Real Estate Specialist (SRES) program to cater to the unique needs of older home buyers and sellers. Home Depot has been conducting pilot tests on senior-oriented independent living programs in some of their outlets. The store plans to be a resource for seniors who want to adapt their homes to their needs as they age.

The impact of people retiring or planning to retire is reflected in the demand for and price of recreational properties across Canada. Many baby boomers are buying recreational homes today with the intention of eventually retiring to them. The industry term for this trend is "recre-retirement" and the market is hot. According to a 2007 Re/max Report, the starting price for a basic recreational property ranges from $75,000 in Newfoundland, to $2.5 million in British Columbia.

The impact of recre-retirement is being felt in all parts of southern B.C., with many Albertans, who are benefiting from the oil boom, leading the charge. In the process, they are inflating prices and changing the rural landscape from the Kootenays to the Sunshine coast.

Already, new retirement and adult lifestyle communities are being developed all across southern and central Ontario. Small and mid-size cities within a two-hour drive of Toronto are predicted to see a spike in population growth once the boomers start to retire. This is a trend that we expect will be duplicated in all major urban areas in Canada. Retirees will be moving from expensive and congested cities to satellite towns within close driving range of the larger city. They will be able to enjoy lower expenses and a more relaxed lifestyle but still be close to the amenities that larger cities can offer. Even moving to smaller, isolated communities will become a better option as technology allows people to stay connected to the wider world.

The housing needs of retirees are clearly different from those of the young and fully employed. There are even differences in the needs of the newly retired versus those of older seniors. Sociologists are predicting intergenerational squabbles as the baby boomers age. This situation is already happening. In retirement homes, a generation gap is forming between residents in their late 60s and early 70s and those in their 80s and 90s. There are clashes over the dress code in the dining rooms, the types of food served, and even the music played at some of the events. The younger retirees want exercise rooms, computer-ready apartments, internet cafes, and better facilities for their more active lifestyle. Many of the older generation do not want such changes, especially if they are forced to pay for the improved amenities. Those in charge of running retirement homes are faced with a dilemma. How can they make their establishments attractive to new and younger residents while at the same time keeping their older residents happy? This will be an even greater challenge in the future. The boomers who do not want the kind of retirement their parents had will certainly not want to live in Mom and Dad's retirement home.

In the future, people who retire will have more housing options than ever before as developers scramble to meet the impending demand. In addition to traditional retirement communities or residences, luxurious facilities featuring hotel-style amenities and services are going up in major cities to appeal to those who want an urban lifestyle. More and more age-restricted communities are being built to serve those who are still working or transitioning into retirement. Residences are being built in established, desirable neighbourhooods for retirees who want to move out of their large homes but still live in the local area where they have their roots.

Typically, as people age and lose some of their physical mobility, they are forced to move to a new home or a residence that is able to accommodate their changing needs. Many seniors will move several times after retirement. Moving is disruptive and stressful and being forced to do so because of deteriorating health makes it even worse. One of the major trends in retirement living is retrofitting homes and setting up retirement communities that allow people to "age in place."

Notwithstanding the excellent retirement communities that are becoming available, most people want to live in their own home after they retire. Homes often require special modifications to allow owners to live safely and independently. These include slip-proof flooring, bath grab bars, levers rather than door handles, and open floor plans. There are even Certified Aging in Place Specialists (CAPS), remodellers who are trained to implement these types of modifications in a home. New housing, based on the principle of universal design, will allow homes to grow and evolve to accommodate the changing needs of their occupants. For example, many homes may be wired with sensors that notify caregivers if the resident is having problems. These types of modifications will allow people to stay in their homes longer and live more independently than was possible before.

More and more retirement homes or communities are being set up to allow their residents to "age in place." Continuing Care Retirement Communities offer different levels of health care and services. A resident might start off in an independent living apartment, then move to assisted living, and later, if necessary, move to a full nursing care facility. The advantage of this type of living arrangement is that people do not have to leave the community. They are able to keep their friends and neighbours and make use of the same facilities.

## What you can do now

- Discuss with your spouse how long you would like to stay in your current home.
- Determine the type of housing you will require in 5, 10, and 20 years.
- Analyze your current home and community. Can you age in place there?
- Research thoroughly any new areas you might wish to live in.
- Keep an open mind to new housing options.

## The bottom line

Everyone will have different housing requirements based on their needs and financial situation. It is important to understand the options and to choose wisely. You need to anticipate the type of housing you will need when your current housing is no longer acceptable. Looking ahead will give you time to understand your future requirements and do the proper research on your next housing option.

# Rule 7

## Develop Realistic Expectations of Your Own Mortality

One of the most basic questions in planning for retirement, especially from a financial perspective, is "When will I die?" Longevity risk—the risk of outliving one's money—is a major concern for most retirees. Retirement planning would, of course, be simplified if we all knew what our lifespans would be. If you knew you were going to live to 75, you would spend and invest your money and live quite differently than if you knew you were going to live to 95. Since you don't know how long you will live, how do you decide what to do with your money? You might plan your retirement based on living to a certain age, draw down your assets to finance your retirement to that age, and then risk running out of money if you live beyond that. On the other hand, if you are cautious and assume you will live to 100 and plan your finances based on that, you may take a pass on spending money on many enjoyable things out of fear that you might need the money later.

What is the solution? Obviously you do not know how long you will live. You can, however, make some educated guesses based on longevity and life expectancy statistics. Your longevity expectations determine your planning horizon—the length of time you use when developing a financial plan.

### LIFE EXPECTANCY TRENDS

Life expectancy is defined as the average number of years a person is expected to live. In 2006, the life expectancy in Canada was 76.9 years for men and 83.7 years for women. A male child born in 2006 has a 50 percent chance of living beyond 76.9 years and a 50 percent chance of dying before that age.

For those who have retired or are expecting to retire soon, knowing how long a child born in 2006 might live, while interesting, does not provide many clues about their own life expectancy. What is more important is the life expectancy at the current age.

The life expectancy at age 65 has risen throughout the past and present century. In 1921, the average age that a 65-year-old man or woman expected to live to was about 78. By 2001, a man of 65 might be expected to live to 82 and a woman to 85.5. In the last 30 years, life expectancy for a 65-year-old has improved by about 1 year for every 10. If that trend persists, the actual life expectancy for a 65-year-old today would be closer to 84 than 82 for a man and 87.5 rather than 85.5 for a woman. An important point to remember is that life expectancy is based on statistics. It includes all those people at age 65, including those who were sick or dying and those who were living an unhealthy lifestyle. A 65-year-old who is fit and living a healthy lifestyle could therefore expect to live a few years longer than the norm.

**TABLE 2.4**
**LIFE EXPECTANCY TRENDS IN CANADA**

| Year | Male | Female |
|------|------|--------|
| 1921 | 58.8 | 60.6 |
| 1931 | 60.0 | 62.1 |
| 1941 | 63.0 | 66.3 |
| 1951 | 66.4 | 70.9 |
| 1961 | 68.4 | 74.3 |
| 1971 | 69.4 | 76.4 |
| 1981 | 72.1 | 79.3 |
| 1991 | 75.5 | 80.9 |
| 2001 | 77.0 | 82.0 |
| 2006 | 76.9 | 83.7 |

Source: Statistics Canada

## PROBABILITIES OF LIVING TO A CERTAIN AGE

Although interesting, these life expectancy figures are still too broad to be much help in determining your planning horizon. A woman of 60 might have a 50 percent chance of living to 85 and a 50 percent chance of living past that age. If she is currently in good health, has good genes, and is following a healthy lifestyle, the odds are even better that she will live past the age of 85. If she bases her financial plan on not living past age 85, she risks outliving her assets.

Another way of looking at life expectancy is to look at probabilities.

**TABLE 2.5**
**PROBABILITY OF REACHING A CERTAIN AGE (PERCENTAGE)**

| Current Age | 80 | | 85 | | 90 | | 95 | | 100 | |
|---|---|---|---|---|---|---|---|---|---|---|
| | M | F | M | F | M | F | M | F | M | F |
| 55 | 52.15 | 67.99 | 32.84 | 50.43 | 15.10 | 29.31 | 4.36 | 11.94 | 0.68 | 2.81 |
| 60 | 54.22 | 69.63 | 34.14 | 51.64 | 15.70 | 30.01 | 4.53 | 12.22 | 0.71 | 2.88 |
| 65 | 57.79 | 72.28 | 36.39 | 53.61 | 16.73 | 31.16 | 4.83 | 12.69 | 0.76 | 2.99 |
| 70 | 64.07 | 76.76 | 40.34 | 56.93 | 18.55 | 33.09 | 5.35 | 13.48 | 0.84 | 3.18 |
| 75 | 75.75 | 84.65 | 47.69 | 62.78 | 21.93 | 36.49 | 6.33 | 14.86 | 0.99 | 3.50 |

Source: Calculated from Statistics Canada, Life Tables 2000–2002

The probabilities of reaching a specific age can provide a better sense of what kind of time horizon to use for planning purposes. For example, a woman of 65 has a 53 percent chance of living to 85, a 31 percent chance of living to 90, and a 12 percent chance of living to 95. A 65-year-old man has a 36 percent chance of living to 85, a 17 percent chance of living to 90, and only a 5 percent chance of living to 95. For those who are fit and genetically blessed and who lead a healthy lifestyle, the probabilities would be higher. A retirement planning horizon of 90 to 95 years for these people at age 65 might be appropriate.

Retirement planning for many people means planning as a couple. The table on page 56 calculates the probabilities of one or both spouses surviving to a certain age. For example, if both spouses are 65, there is a 20 percent chance that both will live to 85 and a 70 percent chance that at least one will live that long. There is only a 5 percent chance that both spouses will survive to the age of 90 but a 42 percent probability that at least one of them will. It would be highly unlikely for both spouses to live to 95 but there is a one in six chance that at least one of them will survive to that age. Again, if both spouses are fit, have good genes, and lead a healthy lifestyle, the probabilities would be higher. It is clear that if such a couple is planning for retirement they should use a planning horizon of at least 95 years.

**TABLE 2.6**

**PROBABILITY OF COUPLE SURVIVAL (PERCENTAGE)**

| Current Age | 80 Both | 80 One | 85 Both | 85 One | 90 Both | 90 One | 95 Both | 95 One | 100 Both | 100 One |
|---|---|---|---|---|---|---|---|---|---|---|
| 55 | 35.46 | 84.69 | 16.56 | 66.70 | 4.43 | 39.98 | 0.52 | 15.77 | 0.02 | 3.48 |
| 60 | 37.75 | 86.09 | 17.63 | 68.15 | 4.71 | 41.00 | 0.55 | 16.20 | 0.02 | 3.57 |
| 65 | 41.77 | 88.30 | 19.51 | 70.49 | 5.21 | 42.68 | 0.61 | 16.90 | 0.02 | 3.73 |
| 70 | 49.18 | 91.65 | 22.96 | 74.30 | 6.14 | 45.50 | 0.72 | 18.11 | 0.03 | 3.99 |
| 75 | 64.12 | 96.28 | 29.94 | 80.53 | 8.00 | 50.42 | 0.94 | 20.25 | 0.03 | 4.46 |

Source: Calculated from Statistics Canada, Life Tables 2000–2002

## What you can do now

- Visualize living a long life.
- Recognize how your needs will change.
- Develop a sense of your own longevity. Do you expect to live longer than people your own age?
- Develop different financial plans assuming different time horizons.

## The bottom line

If you are fit, maintain a normal body weight, lead a healthy lifestyle, and have long-living parents and grandparents, you can expect to live well past the average life expectancy. A planning horizon for your retirement planning should be about 30 years long. In other words, your financial plan should assume that you will need money until age 95.

# Part 3

## Calculate Your Cost of Living in Retirement

FOR MOST RETIREES, THERE IS A FINE LINE BETWEEN SPENDING TOO MUCH AND TOO LITTLE. Retirees who spend too much, especially in the early years, run the risk of depleting their savings before they die. Alternatively, retirees who spend too little will needlessly do without many pleasures and comforts because they fear they will run out of money in their old age. These individuals will die with a larger estate, but the money will do them no good when they are in their graves. There is an optimal balance between spending too much and doing without. A major challenge of retirement planning is to find this optimal balance. The process of estimating your cost of living in retirement is a good first step.

Financial security should be one of your most important goals. It can be measured using a personal income statement and a personal balance sheet. In your overall financial picture your liabilities and expenses are just as important as your assets and income. If you run out of money while in retirement, it does not really matter if it was because you spent too much or because your investment assets were mismanaged and did not provide sufficient income and growth. The net result is the same—in your final years you may be living in poverty or, at best, much-reduced circumstances.

In the financial services industry, most planners pay too little attention to spending or expenses. They either rely on the client to make a rough guess at his spending requirements, or use a rule of thumb, such as "to maintain your lifestyle in retirement will require 75 percent of your pre-retirement income." Most planners will assume that expenses will go up each year by the same rate as that of inflation. The underlying assumption is that "real" spending does not change in retirement. It will be the same whether you are 65, 85, or 100.

Financial planners typically spend most of their time and effort on the income and financial side of a client's balance sheet. Most planners will say that achieving financial goals in retirement is determined by how investments, rather than personal finances and spending, are managed. Very few planners are knowledgeable about the spending and expense patterns of retirees, but all profess to be experts on investing. However, in order to have a financially secure retirement, the proper management of your budget is just as important as the proper management of your investment portfolio.

In the real world, most retirees will adjust their spending to reflect changes in their income, wealth, age, objectives, and the success or failure of their investment strategy. In other words, they adjust their standard of living to reflect changes in their lives and finances. Retirees generally do not let their lifestyle choices drive their investment strategy. This is an important distinction that you need to understand. Retirees will generally adopt a lifestyle or standard of living that can be supported by their finances; they are smart enough not to try to make their finances fit their lifestyle.

# Rule 8

## Estimate Your Spending in the Early Years of Retirement

For the financial planning process to be effective, you need to know how much you are spending. It is particularly important to get an accurate handle on what you will spend during the first few years in retirement. Understanding spending requirements is the main consideration in estimating how much capital you will need. Rough estimates are not good enough because mistakes made now may mean the difference between a financially successful retirement and one that is a failure. Research shows that people who carefully estimated their spending needs pre-retirement were better prepared than those who did not, and as we noted earlier, preparation is one of the important factors that determine satisfaction in retirement. Like most everything else in life, the more work you put into something, the better the results will be.

### LIFESTYLE CHOICES

The first step in estimating your spending requirements is to determine the type of lifestyle you want. Will it be similar to your pre-retirement lifestyle minus the work? Will it change dramatically as a result of moving to a different part of the country, downsizing to a smaller home, or taking up expensive hobbies and leisure-time activities? Will you spend more time travelling? Will you be working, starting a new business, or doing volunteer work? How will you spend your time on a day-to-day basis?

Most people's lifestyle does not change dramatically from pre-retirement to post-retirement. Typically, retirees stay in the same home and continue enjoying the same activities. However, one of the dangers people face as they approach retirement is "lifestyle creep," a phenomenon Michael Stein discusses in an article published in the *Journal of Financial Planning*. Five to ten years before retirement, people are typically in their peak earning years. At the same time, many of the expenses they had earlier, such as paying off a mortgage, raising a family, or financing a child's post-secondary education, have ended or been reduced dramatically. Faced with a surplus of cash, some people buy more expensive cars, more expensive vacations, or even a second home rather than putting the money aside for retirement.

Since a common retirement goal is to maintain the lifestyle enjoyed in the last few years of employment, retirees who have spent freely in the past few years will require more funds to support their new, more lavish lifestyles. Unfortunately, they won't have the resources to do this, since they spent their surplus cash before they retired.

## ESTIMATING EXPENSES AND SPENDING IN RETIREMENT

Monitoring your current expenses and estimating what your expenses will be once you have retired will allow you to make financial and budgeting decisions with confidence and will improve your odds of having a financially successful retirement. If possible, begin this process at least three years before retiring.

To make a retirement expense estimate, focus on your spending needs during the first few years in retirement. Typically, spending is highest at this time. An estimate for these years provides a base for calculating expenses in later years. Start by analyzing your current expenses, then adjust those expenses to reflect how your spending patterns will change once you are retired. These are some of the factors to keep in mind as you plan:

CHILDREN: Typically, children have moved out of the family home, but there is a trend of "boomerang" adult children moving back home, which can add unforeseen expenses.

WORK-RELATED EXPENSES: Earning a living can cost money. Costs such as public transit or car-related expenses, employment insurance, office attire, dry cleaning, union dues, work lunches, and gifts to co-workers all disappear once you are retired.

HOUSE AND HOME: Typically, people have paid off their mortgage and completed major household improvements by the time they retire.

LEISURE TIME: With more free time available, spending might increase for hobbies, travelling, and recreational activities. However, you can save money by doing these things during non-peak seasons.

**HEALTH AND FITNESS:** Poor health and lack of fitness might result in higher health-related costs. However, the curtailment of some physical activities may result in lower expenses. For instance, people who skied at an earlier age might not be able to do so when they retire because of an injury or disability.

**TIME VERSUS MONEY:** When you are working, time is valuable and you incur many expenses in order to save time—for example, eating out rather than preparing a meal at home, or paying someone to walk the dog or clean the house. In retirement, time is cheap and money is valuable. People have more time to prepare meals, clip coupons, or look for price savings on their purchases.

**SAVINGS:** Prior to retirement, a sizable portion of income goes to saving for this time of life, whether it is paying off the mortgage, putting money in an RRSP, or contributing to a company pension plan, CPP, or other savings account. Once you retire, the need to save for retirement is eliminated.

**TAXES:** The lower the income, the lower the income tax. Tax reductions in retirement can be significant. Pension income can now be split, whereas salary income could not.

**SPENDING ADJUSTMENTS:** People's spending adjusts naturally to their income and wealth. When income rises, people spend more, and when it drops, they spend less. People can be very resourceful in cutting expenses when necessary.

**UNCERTAINTY:** Uncertainty about how much money they will require in retirement and how long they will live tends to make most people spend less.

**BEQUESTS:** Many retirees will spend less on themselves because they want to leave an inheritance to their children or a gift to charity.

**PROPENSITY TO SPEND:** The older people get, the less materialistic they become. They get less enjoyment out of spending, so they end up spending less. As B.B. King would say, "The thrill is gone."

**AGE DISCOUNTS:** Many businesses offer special deals or other benefits to seniors and all levels of government offer subsidized programs for the elderly.

## CATEGORIZING EXPENDITURES

Although there are different ways to itemize expenditures, we like to base ours on the categories Statistics Canada uses to calculate the Consumer Price Index (CPI). By using this system you can compare your individual spending patterns to the statistical averages of other Canadians.

**FOOD:** In this category, you would include food, alcohol, and sundry items for consumption in the home as well as restaurant meals and takeout food. Once people retire, home food costs are usually lower; as people age, they generally eat smaller portions. Also, with more time to prepare meals, they cook at home more often and spend less money on takeout and restaurant food.

**SHELTER:** Shelter costs include rent, mortgage payments, property taxes, maintenance and repairs, home insurance, water, fuel, and electricity. If you are living in the same home after retiring, your shelter costs should remain fairly constant. Most seniors have paid off the mortgage by the time they retire. Being at home more often means utilities charges will increase slightly. But in some jurisdictions, property taxes are lower for seniors. Of course, moving, downsizing, or buying a second home after retirement would change these costs dramatically.

**HOUSEHOLD OPERATIONS:** These are the costs related to running the household—telephone and internet, domestic services, cleaning products, landscaping products and services, furniture and appliances. Normally these expenses should not change dramatically for new retirees. People who paid for housecleaning or landscaping services while they were employed could see a reduction in expenses if they take over these tasks themselves. Others might have to pay for these services because they are unable to do them themselves. Typically, retirees do not spend money on new furniture; however, appliances might require replacing from time to time.

**CLOTHING:** This category includes clothes, shoes, accessories, and jewellery. Since casual clothing is generally less expensive than work clothing, these costs tend to decline throughout retirement.

**TRANSPORTATION:** This includes the purchasing and leasing of private vehicles, gasoline, repairs and maintenance, insurance, and registration. It would also include intercity transportation and bus, train, and air travel. Transportation can be a major cost, especially if you live in a large city and have a long commute. In retirement, most of the regular costs of commuting are eliminated. Car insurance costs are lower when you are driving for recreation rather than driving to and from work. For those who used to have long daily drives while employed, costs can come down significantly in retirement, reflecting not only lower gasoline costs but also lower car maintenance and repair costs. A car that gets used less frequently does not have to be replaced as often. But when estimating automotive expenses, don't forget that all cars eventually need to be replaced. If you travel a lot during retirement, other expenses such as air fares and long-distance driving costs can increase. However, with more time to plan a trip and more flexibility in determining when to go, you can get considerably lower air fares.

**HEALTH AND PERSONAL CARE:** The cost of health care, prescription and non-prescription drugs, dental care, and personal care supplies and services should not change much in the first few years of retirement. These expenses will increase later.

**RECREATION:** This includes recreational equipment and services, home entertainment equipment, travel services, including accommodations and tours, tickets for sports and cultural events, as well as cablevision, books, newspapers, and magazines. These are strictly discretionary items. Whether the expenses for these items go up or down in retirement depends on your lifestyle. If money is tight, these types of expenses can be cut back.

**GIFTS:** Gifts to family, church, and charitable causes are another area that is strictly discretionary. Seniors are usually generous and do not necessarily cut back on gifts and donations, even if their income is lower.

**ONE-TIME OR INFREQUENT EXPENSES:** One of the biggest mistakes people make when estimating their expenses is forgetting or underestimating irregular but significant costs. These expenses can include a new car or RV, a one-time trip, or major dental work or cosmetic surgery. Often they include a large, one-time sum of money to a child for a wedding, a down payment on a house, or a major home repair.

It is important to incorporate these irregular but large-ticket items into your overall spending estimates. One approach is to convert the one-time expenditures into annual or monthly estimates. For example, if you plan to buy a new car every five years at a cost of $30,000 including your trade-in, you would add $6,000 a year or $500 a month to your spending estimates. Estimate each major purchase within the first 10 years of retirement. Let's assume that includes a car, a trip to Europe, a new roof, and a cash gift to a child for a total of $72,000. You would have to set aside $7,200 a year or $600 a month. One way to ensure you save this money is to create what accountants call a "sinking fund." You set aside a certain amount separate from your investments or savings, or pay a monthly amount into a separate account to fund those expenses.

## ESTIMATE TARGET EXPENSES VERSUS ESSENTIAL EXPENSES

Just to warn you—it will take some time to estimate your spending requirements in the first years of retirement, but it is vital that you do so. The spending estimate should be based on what you believe is reasonable, given your expected financial situation and expected lifestyle. After completing the first estimate, if the forecast seems achievable and you are happy with the results, it will provide a target budget.

Once you complete the first estimate, repeat the exercise. Only this time, when reviewing the expenses, look for those expenditures that could be reduced without diminishing your quality of life. If money were a little tight, what budget items could you easily cut out entirely? The gym membership that you seldom use? A new car every eight years rather than every five years? The trip to Europe? Rather than treat yourself to an expensive restaurant every month, could you switch to a more moderately priced one instead?

By reviewing the budget with cost-cutting in mind you will accomplish a number of things. First, you will establish spending priorities. What are the important items that you cannot cut back on? Second, you will free up money that you could use on other parts of your budget. Third, if you have to reduce spending for an unexpected reason, you will have a plan in place. As income and wealth from investments fluctuate in retirement and unexpected expenses occur, most retirees make adjustments by cutting back those items that have a lower priority.

The table below is an example of an expense summary.

### TABLE 3.1
### ANNUAL ESTIMATED EXPENDITURES (NOT INCLUDING INCOME TAX)

|  | Target ($) | Essential ($) | Discretionary ($) |
|---|---|---|---|
| Regular | 30,000 | 25,000 | 5,000 |
| Infrequent | 10,000 | 5,000 | 5,000 |
| Total | 40,000 | 30,000 | 10,000 |

The difference between target and essential spending estimates is discretionary spending—expenses that are desirable but not necessary. The target spending estimate is made up of money you need to spend and money you would like to spend. Although income tax may be a large expense, it is not included at this point because most financial planning programs use an estimate for expenses (before tax) and then calculate the tax on income from all sources.

Usually essential spending and target spending both go up as wealth and income increase . However, more and more money will be spent on discretionary versus non-discretionary items. For seniors with limited resources and income, target spending estimates will be close to their essential needs. Many seniors who rely strictly on Old Age Security and Guaranteed Income Supplement for their income in retirement *might* see their income drop below the level required to sustain their most basic needs.

## TABLE 3.2
### TARGET AND ESSENTIAL EXPENSES

| | Target Expenses | Essential Expenses | Discretionary Expenses |
|---|---|---|---|
| **FOOD** | | | |
| Eating at home | | | |
| Meals in restaurants | | | |
| Alcohol | | | |
| Pet food and supplies | | | |
| | | | |
| **SHELTER** | | | |
| Rent | | | |
| Mortgage | | | |
| Property taxes | | | |
| Maintenance & repairs | | | |
| Home Insurance | | | |
| Water | | | |
| Heating and cooling | | | |
| Electricity | | | |
| | | | |
| **HOUSEHOLD OPERATIONS** | | | |
| Telephone | | | |
| Internet | | | |
| Domestic services | | | |
| Cleaning products | | | |
| Landscaping | | | |
| Furniture & appliances | | | |
| | | | |
| **CLOTHING** | | | |
| Clothing | | | |
| Footwear | | | |
| Miscellaneous | | | |

## TRANSPORTATION (VEHICLES)

Purchase _____ _____ _____

Leasing _____ _____ _____

Gasoline _____ _____ _____

Repairs & maintenance _____ _____ _____

Insurance _____ _____ _____

Registration _____ _____ _____

## OTHER TRANSPORTATION

Intercity _____ _____ _____

Bus or rail _____ _____ _____

Air _____ _____ _____

## HEALTH AND PERSONAL CARE

Prescription drugs _____ _____ _____

Eye care _____ _____ _____

Dental care _____ _____ _____

Personal care _____ _____ _____

Pet care _____ _____ _____

## RECREATION

Home entertainment _____ _____ _____

Travel & vacation _____ _____ _____

Cultural events & sports _____ _____ _____

Reading materials _____ _____ _____

Education _____ _____ _____

## GIFTS

Family _____ _____ _____

Church _____ _____ _____

Charities _____ _____ _____

## What you can do now

- Gather up your bank statements, credit card statements, and other receipts. Do a detailed breakdown of your current expenses and analyze your spending patterns.
- Develop a budget for the first year of retirement, recognizing how your spending patterns will change after you stop working.
- Break down your spending into what you need and what you want.
- Identify major one-time expenses over the next 10 years.
- Make major purchases while you are still working.

## The bottom line

There is an optimal balance between saving and spending. If you spend too much, especially in the early years of retirement, you risk running out of money. If you are too cautious and overly concerned about your financial security, you may end up not enjoying your retirement to the fullest extent possible. Developing a good understanding of your spending requirements, particularly during the first couple of years in retirement, is an important step in the planning process.

# Rule 9

## Keep Track of Expenses the Easy Way

Most people have a good sense of their income and net worth. They are constantly reminded of it when they pay their taxes and read their regular bank and investment statements. But many people have only a vague idea of how much money they spend and what they spend it on. To understand your expenses, you need to analyze and monitor your spending habits. The better the "spending" information you have, the better you will be able to meet your retirement goals and the easier it will be to manage your finances confidently.

Adding up receipts and bills can be a tedious job. But the information you gain from analyzing expenses is critical, so this is a step you must not skip. The task can also be made much easier with a simple reorganization of your finances. By following the three-step method below, you will be able to calculate your annual expenses in five minutes, once a year. You can perform a more detailed breakdown in an hour.

### STEP 1: HAVE ONE BANK ACCOUNT FOR ALL YOUR EXPENSES

This is the most important step. Set up one bank account for household and lifestyle expenses. This will be the only bank account you use for credit card payments, utilities charges, debit card transactions, groceries, charitable donations, and even your "walking around" spending money. You will not use funds from this bank account for investment purposes or for income tax payments but only for lifestyle and household expenses.

You will not make cheque, cash, or automatic deposits to this account. You will make these deposits to another account that you set up to handle deposits or savings. The amount that goes into your "spending" account will be relatively large or regular transfers from your "savings" account. The goal is to make only a small number of deposits to your spending account each year so that it's easy to calculate their total. For example, if you estimate your annual expenses to be $36,000 per year, you could make equal deposits of $3,000 per month or $9,000 per quarter. A one-time large purchase would be paid out of this account as well. If the purchase price of a car was $33,432 including all taxes, then a one-time payment for that amount would be deposited into the account. By using this method, you will be able to determine very easily how much money you deposit.

To keep track of your expenses, use a credit card or a debit card, make online payments, or use automatic debiting for as many purchases and expenses as possible. This is an easier way to keep track of detailed expenses than rounding up receipts. Make sure to keep your bank statements and credit card statements in order.

## STEP 2: CALCULATE YOUR TOTAL EXPENSES FOR THE YEAR

If you set up your account properly, you need only three pieces of information to calculate the total expenses paid for the year. These are the beginning of the year opening balance, the total amount deposited, and the balance at the end of the year.

Calculating your total annual expenses is a good start; if you did nothing but this, you would have better information than most people. However, more detail will make your expense information more useful.

### TABLE 3.3
### TOTAL EXPENSES, 2008

| | | |
|---|---|---|
| Opening balance Dec. 31, 2007 | | 4,321.00 |
| Total deposited to account | 12 x $3,000 plus $5,000 one-time deposit | + 41,000.00 |
| Total funds available | | 45,321.00 |
| Closing balance Dec. 31, 2008 | | − 6,428.00 |
| Total expenses (funds available less closing balance) | | $38,893.00 |

## STEP 3: DETERMINE DETAIL EXPENSES

You don't need to keep track of every single entry or expense. The idea is to itemize the regular and the large expenses and differentiate between those that are essential and those that are discretionary. An expenditure can have both an essential and a discretionary component. For example, if you budgeted for a $30,000 car but bought a $40,000 one instead, then $30,000 is essential and $10,000 is discretionary.

First, itemize all the expenses that you pay on a regular schedule— monthly utilities, club dues, or annual items such as property taxes and insurance. The annual expenses for monthly or quarterly regular payments can be easily calculated. Those that are based on usage (phone bills and utilities) can be estimated. Although most of these items would be considered essential, some might be discretionary.

Other regular expenses such as gasoline, food, haircuts, dry cleaning, dog grooming, and pet food can be calculated by taking a sample of these costs over a two- or three-month period and then estimating them for a year. Like the first grouping of expenses, most will be essential or basic, but some may be considered discretionary.

You will also have expenses that are not part of your regular, day-to-day, month-to-month, or even year-to-year costs. Major home renovations, car repairs, a special trip, new furniture, dental work, or a new pet are examples. Go through your chequing accounts and credit card statements to identify these expenses. Like the others, they can be separated into essential and discretionary amounts.

Table 3.4 is an example of a detailed spending summary. In this example, we itemized $35,660 in detailed expenses. Note that there is $3,233 in unallocated expenses that can be added to whatever category seems appropriate.

### TABLE 3.4
### DETAILED SPENDING SUMMARY, 2008

|  | Essential $ | Discretionary $ | Total $ |
| --- | --- | --- | --- |
| Food | 6,525 | 235 | 6,760 |
| Shelter | 8,807 | 0 | 8,807 |
| Household operations | 2,309 | 0 | 2,309 |
| Household furnishings | 1,046 | 537 | 1,583 |
| Clothing | 1,569 | 250 | 1,819 |
| Transportation | 5,479 | 1,825 | 7,304 |
| Health | 2,268 | 0 | 2,268 |
| Personal | 743 | 0 | 743 |
| Recreation | 1,434 | 1,500 | 2,934 |
| Reading | 303 | 0 | 303 |
| Gifts | 831 | 0 | 831 |
| Total allocated | 31,313 | 4,347 | 35,660 |
| Unallocated expenses |  |  | + 3,233 |
| Total expenses |  |  | $38,893 |

Of course, many of your essential expenses can be reduced. Eliminating one car or downsizing and moving into a smaller home can result in significant savings. Same basic expenses are not in fact essential in the long term but are due to lifestyle choices.

## What you can do now

- Set up one bank account for all your expenses.
- Rearrange your banking practices to allow you to track income, savings, and investment and expenses easily.
- Every year, determine how you spend your money.

## The bottom line

Budgeting and monitoring expenses is important for the financial management of any household, but it becomes even more critical when you are retired and on a fixed income. You can follow these practices easily if you pay all your household expenses out of one account and perform a good detailed accounting of annual expenses every year.

# Rule 10

## Be Prepared for Your Spending Patterns to Change as You Age

As we age, most of us go through a series of major life events. These events include getting our first job, settling down with a partner, buying a house, having a child, retiring, etc. At each stage, we develop new goals as we address the different challenges and opportunities. As our lives change, our income level changes, and we develop new needs. These changing priorities and income are reflected in how we save, spend, and invest our money.

In retirement, spending patterns will change again, reflecting, among other things, typically lower levels of income, the elimination of expenses related to work, more free time, and changing health. Not only do our spending patterns change after retirement—our expenditures and consumption change during different phases of retirement as we age. A 65-year-old has different spending patterns than an 85-year-old.

A common and serious fault with most financial planning efforts is the assumption that spending in "real" dollars is more or less constant throughout retirement. According to this assumption, expenses will consistently increase by the underlying rate of inflation. In reality, studies suggest that "real" retirement spending generally declines at a more or less constant rate throughout retirement.

### SPENDING PATTERNS IN RETIREMENT

In his paper "Change in Expenditure Patterns of Older Households in Canada, 1982–2003," Raj Chawla of Statistics Canada examined how both income and spending changes for seniors in different age groups. Chawla's analysis of spending patterns provides useful insights for those who are planning their retirement and want to estimate how their spending requirements might change. The findings of the study were based on the 2003 Survey of Household Spending. Although the survey looked at spending patterns among unattached men and women as well as couples, we will concentrate only on the findings for couples.

The study analyzed people in three different age groups: 55 to 64, 65 to 74, and 75 and older. As would be expected, income dropped from the youngest group to the next, reflecting the greater percentage of those in the older group who were not earning any income from work. Income fell again for those over 75. Not surprisingly, spending and taxes were lower for the older seniors. Security, which represents payments to pension plans, employment insurance, and life insurance, dropped as well.

TABLE 3.5

HOUSEHOLD SPENDING BY SENIOR COUPLES, 2003

| Age | 55–64 | 65–74 | 75+ |
| --- | --- | --- | --- |
| Mean income | $66,166 | $45,757 | $36,257 |
| Consumption | 44,391 | 33,726 | 25,913 |
| Income tax | 14,358 | 7,321 | 4,061 |
| Security | 3,308 | 1,235 | 363 |
| Gifts | 1,919 | 1,556 | 2,212 |
| Savings | 2,250 | 1,922 | 3,734 |

Source: Statistics Canada Survey of Household Spending, 2003

What *is* surprising is the fact that money allocated for savings and gifts actually increased for those 75 and older. For this group, the amount spent on gifts to family and charity increased to $2,212, up $600 from the 64 to 75 age group. Also, savings rose to $3,734, over $1,800 higher than the 64 to 75 age group. In spite of having less income, those over 75 are saving more than younger seniors.

The results of this study suggest two things: seniors not only spend less as their income decreases (which is what we would expect), but as they get older, they voluntarily spend less regardless of their income. A more detailed analysis of these spending patterns helps explain why this happens.

## HOW SENIORS SPEND THEIR MONEY

The detailed consumption trends in the following table show that seniors' spending drops across the board for all the main categories of expenses.

In the 65 to 74 age group, the main expense items were shelter, transportation, food, and recreation, which represented almost 70 percent of total expenditures. For those couples 75 and over, the major expense items were shelter, food, transportation, and health. Recreation was considerably less important. These top four expenses represented about 73 percent of total expenditures. As you can see, priorities and needs shift as people age, and this is reflected in the change in their spending patterns.

TABLE 3.6
DETAILED CONSUMPTION BY SENIOR COUPLES, 2003

| Age | 55-64 | 65-74 | 75+ |
| --- | --- | --- | --- |
| Food | 6,661 | 6,145 | 5,092 |
| Shelter | 10,185 | 8,006 | 7,287 |
| Household operations | 2,600 | 2,099 | 1,827 |
| Household furnishings | 2,091 | 1,439 | 1,051 |
| Clothing | 2,452 | 1,654 | 1,060 |
| Transportation | 9,848 | 6,640 | 4,344 |
| Health | 2,262 | 2,062 | 2,102 |
| Personal | 773 | 675 | 568 |
| Recreation | 3,907 | 2,667 | 994 |
| Reading | 329 | 275 | 243 |
| Tobacco & alcohol | 1,598 | 933 | 656 |
| Miscellaneous | 1,479 | 1,024 | 646 |
| Average consumption | $44,391 | $33,726 | $25,913 |

Source: Statistics Canada Survey of Household Spending, 2003

The difference in spending for housing and shelter between the two younger groups can likely be attributed to mortgages that have been paid off or to downsizing. The further drop in spending for shelter in the oldest group is most likely a result of further downsizing.

The largest decline in spending was in transportation—almost 30 percent of the total difference in spending between the youngest and oldest groups. The former were still paying costs related to the daily commute to and from work, while the latter may have stopped driving altogether and no longer owned cars. As people age, they tend to travel less.

In spite of having more time for recreation, seniors' spending tends to drop with age in part due to poor health and fitness or lack of mobility. Food costs also decrease in the older groups, reflecting fewer restaurant visits as well as smaller appetites.

All these changes in spending among the three age groups reflect a different pattern between discretionary and non-discretionary spending. The basic needs—food, shelter, health care, and household expenses—showed lower than average percentage changes, while the more discretionary items—furniture, clothing, transportation, and recreation—showed larger than average drops. It also appears that, as people age, money they save from reduced costs, such as eliminating a car, does not go into increased spending on items for themselves, but rather into additional savings or gifts.

## What you can do now

- Visualize the future and recognize how your financial needs will change as you age.
- Recognize the fact that discretionary spending will decrease.
- Assume that spending in "real terms" will go down for transportation, recreation, and food.
- Assume that spending in "real terms" for health care will rise.
- Factor in spending increases that will be 1 or 2 percent lower per year than the underlying rate of inflation.
- Redo your financial plan using different spending patterns in retirement.

## The bottom line

When planning and preparing for retirement, you should factor in a lower level of spending as you get older. This will allow you to have more confidence in your financial security and to spend more money in the earlier years of retirement when you can enjoy it the most.

# Rule 11

## Don't Underestimate the Impact Even Low Inflation Can Have on Your Cost of Living

We all face two big risks in retirement: longevity risk, the danger of running out of money before we die, and inflation risk, the steady erosion of our money's purchasing power. For those living on a fixed income, inflation should be a primary concern. The greater the rate of inflation, the more money you will require to buy the same basic necessities. In turn, high inflation dramatically increases the longevity risk for those on a fixed income. This is an even bigger concern today because we are all living longer.

Most of the last 20 years has been a period of historically low inflation, so people do not have the same concern about it as they did in the 1990s and early 1980s. However, even low rates of inflation can seriously erode the financial well-being of retirees who live a long life. A period of unexpectedly high inflation, such as we experienced in the 1970s and early 1980s, would be devastating for those living on a fixed income. If a diversified investment portfolio loses 20 percent in a bear market, in time it will normally make up those losses and continue to appreciate to higher levels. But if retirees lose 20 percent of their purchasing power to inflation, it is essentially money that is lost forever. One of the most important financial goals in retirement is to protect the purchasing power of your assets and income.

### HISTORICAL INFLATION RATES

Inflation levels since the end of the Second World War have been volatile, with annual inflation rates ranging from close to zero to double digits. Looking at some of the inflation rates in the postwar period provides some insight into what we might expect in the future. However, we do not offer any inflation forecasts; we will leave that to the economists.

The table on page 80 looks at average annual inflation rates in Canada as measured by the Consumer Price Index (CPI) over 5- 10- 20- and 30-year time frames.

With increased longevity, the time spent in retirement could be 20 to 30 years. Over those longer time frames, any volatility in the inflation rates tends to be smoothed out, but it can still be quite high. Over a 20-year period, the average annual CPI inflation rates varied between 2 percent and 7 percent. For the longer 30-year period, which would be the normal time frame for someone retiring at age 60 and dying at age 90, the annual inflation rate varied between 3 percent and just over 5.5 percent. In the next 20 to 30 years, it is conceivable that the inflation rate could average from 3 to 5 percent, a rate considerably higher than we have experienced in the last 10 to 15 years. Although 3 to 5 percent does not seem that high, these rates compounded for 20 to 30 years can have a dramatic effect on the purchasing power of the dollar.

TABLE 3.7
AVERAGE ANNUAL INFLATION RATES (PERCENTAGE)

| Period Ending | 5 Yrs | 10 Yrs | 20 Yrs | 30 Yrs |
|---|---|---|---|---|
| 1966 | 2.44 | 1.95 | 3.08 | 2.84 |
| 1971 | 3.78 | 3.11 | 2.03 | 3.07 |
| 1976 | 8.39 | 6.06 | 3.98 | 4.07 |
| 1981 | 10.18 | 9.28 | 6.15 | 4.36 |
| 1986 | 5.20 | 7.66 | 6.86 | 5.17 |
| 1991 | 4.42 | 4.99 | 7.02 | 5.66 |
| 1996 | 1.59 | 3.00 | 5.30 | 5.61 |
| 2001 | 1.65 | 1.62 | 3.20 | 5.31 |
| 2006 | 2.35 | 2.00 | 2.50 | 4.33 |
| 2007 | 2.31 | 1.98 | 2.48 | 4.16 |

Source: Bank of Canada

Fortunately, the Old Age Security program and Canada Pension Plan are indexed to the underlying rate of inflation as measured by the CPI. Those who have private pensions indexed to inflation receive additional inflation protection. Most retirees, however, will have to take proactive steps with their investments to protect the integrity of their financial assets from the effect of inflation.

The rate of inflation as measured by the CPI is quite broad and can vary depending on your spending patterns and where you live. For example, when gasoline prices rose dramatically from 2005 to 2008, those who used their cars for long commutes saw their cost of living increase significantly, while those who did not own a car did not. Those who bought a first home in the hot real estate market of 2003 to 2007 saw a large increase in their cost of living compared to those who already owned their home.

### TABLE 3.8
### AMOUNT REQUIRED TO MAINTAIN PURCHASING POWER OF $10,000

| Annual Inflation Rate | 5 Yrs | 10 Yrs | 20 Yrs | 30 Yrs |
|---|---|---|---|---|
| 2 | $11,041 | $12,190 | $14,859 | $18,114 |
| 3 | 11,593 | 13,439 | 18,061 | 24,273 |
| 4 | 12,167 | 14,802 | 21,911 | 32,434 |
| 5 | 12,763 | 16,289 | 26,533 | 43,219 |
| 6 | 13,382 | 17,908 | 32,071 | 57,435 |
| 7 | 14,026 | 19,672 | 38,697 | 76,123 |
| 8 | 14,693 | 21,589 | 46,610 | 100,627 |
| 9 | 15,386 | 23,674 | 56,044 | 132,677 |
| 10 | 16,105 | 25,937 | 67,275 | 174,494 |

Looking forward, it is hard to predict what the inflation rate will be and what will cause the most significant cost of living increases. But we can use some demographic clues to make guesses about how a senior's cost-of-living expenses might be affected in the future. It is estimated that the number of people over the age of 65 will increase by 34.7 percent by 2016 and by 86.8 percent by 2026 over the 2006 numbers. This large increase in the number of retirees will create greater demand for products and services that are very specific to the seniors' market. With baby boomers starting to retire in large numbers, the resulting labour shortage will bid up the cost of labour, adding to inflationary pressures.

In the area of health and health care, the increase in demand compounds the problem of an increase in costs due to potential labour shortages. Baby boomer doctors, nurses, technicians, administrators, and other medical professionals and skilled tradespeople are going to retire just when we need them the most. There is a very high probability that inflation in health-care costs will have a negative impact on seniors, either through an increase in health-care premiums, a shortage of health-care workers, poorer service, higher costs for home care, or greater cost for extended care facilities.

## What you can do now

- Ensure that part of your investments provide a hedge against inflation. Inflation hedges include stock market investments, real return bonds, and real assets including gold, commodities, and real estate.

## The bottom line

For most working people, inflation is not an issue, because wages generally increase faster than the underlying rate of inflation. (We say generally because, although the situation reflects underlying wage growth and wages that increase due to seniority and promotions, not everyone benefits.) For retirees on a fixed income, inflation becomes a much more important concern. This is especially the case today, when people are living 20 to 30 years after retirement. Over such an extended period of time, even modest inflation can dramatically reduce the purchasing power of someone on a fixed income.

# Part 4

## Calculate Your Retirement Income

IF YOU ARE PLANNING TO RETIRE BUT DON'T KNOW IF YOU WILL HAVE ENOUGH INCOME, YOU are likely to move into this next phase of your life with fear and anxiety rather than joyful anticipation. One way to become more confident about the future is to make a realistic calculation of your expected income.

In Canada, the retirement income system is considered to be composed of three pillars. The first pillar comprises the Old Age Security (OAS) program and the Guaranteed Income Supplement (GIS) program, which provide a universal pension for all Canadians, especially those on a low income. The second pillar is made up of the Canada Pension Plan (CPP) and the Quebec Pension Plan (QPP), universal plans for all working Canadians. The third pillar consists of Registered Pension Plans and Registered Retirement Savings Plans (RRSPs).

In reality, many retirees have seven pillars. In addition to the above three, they might have income from a job, income from savings, income from the equity in a home, and financial support and an inheritance from family. Not everyone will have funds from these additional sources, but for those who do, the amounts can be significant, and retirees should consider them when estimating income.

TABLE 4.1

AVERAGE INCOME BREAKDOWN FOR SENIORS, 2003

|  | Men | % Receiving | Women | % Receiving |
|---|---|---|---|---|
| Earnings | $9,900 | 25.1 | $8,100 | 10.9 |
| Investment income | 4,800 | 56.1 | 4,500 | 58.4 |
| Retirement income | 17,900 | 69.8 | 10,200 | 53.0 |
| OAS/GIS | 6,100 | 93.6 | 6,700 | 97.4 |
| CPP/QPP | 6,500 | 95.8 | 4,900 | 85.8 |

Source: Statistics Canada, Survey of Consumer Finances; Survey of Labour and Income Dynamics

In 2003, Statistics Canada analyzed sources of income for seniors. Not surprisingly, most seniors relied on government programs for a portion of their income, with 90 percent of all seniors receiving CPP/QPP and/or

# Identifying Sources of Income

In his early 60s, Paul returned to Canada to retire after a long career as a missionary in Africa. Soon after Paul and his wife, Anna, got settled they began to experience inflation shock. As they realized that they could not live on their small church pension, they began to panic. They felt certain that they were going to end up in abject poverty, without enough even for basic necessities.

Even though Paul had no savings of any kind, he came to us for help. We knew he needed a financial plan, and we started by adding up the various sources of income that he and Anna would have at age 65. We then looked at the amount that they wanted to spend in the early years of their retirement and the lower amount they planned to spend in their later years. It turned out that Paul also planned to work part-time in the ministry for at least five years. Anna expected to earn $200 per week giving piano lessons to children in her neighbourhood.

We calculated their family income, which consisted of their Old Age Security pension, their Canada Pension Plan payments, and their Guaranteed Income Supplement, plus their church pension and the projected income from part-time employment. We calculated their expected expenses until Paul turned 75 and their expenses for the rest of their lives after that. When we put it all together, the plan showed that instead of running out of money and living in poverty, this retired couple actually had enough to live comfortably and take a small vacation each year. They had to see it to believe it. Once the planning process was started and the facts became clear, the solutions also became obvious.

OAS/GIS. The largest source for many people was income from a private pension or RRSP. The average retirement income was $17,900 for men and $10,200 for women. Slightly more than 25 percent of men and 10 percent of women received income from some form of employment. Some retirees received income from all of these sources while others received income from only a few.

# Rule 12

## Be Sure to Collect What You Are Entitled to from Government Programs

Canada's social safety net ensures that all Canadians can enjoy at least a basic level of financial security during their retirement. This was not always the case. Before the Old Age Pension Act of 1927, most seniors had to work or rely on their family or savings to provide support in their old age.

Today, the government entitlements are large and expensive programs. In 2006, over 31 billion dollars was paid out in Old Age Security pensions, including the Guaranteed Income Supplement. The Canada Pension Plan, exclusive of the Quebec Pension Plan, paid out over 25 billion dollars in 2006, including retirement, disability, and survivors' benefits. The Old Age Security program and the Canada Pension Plan form the foundation for most retirees' incomes. For some seniors, these programs represent their only source of income. Understanding these programs is an important part of everyone's retirement planning.

### OLD AGE SECURITY

WHO IS ELIGIBLE? The Old Age Security pension is a monthly payment available to most Canadians 65 or older. You must apply to receive the benefits. If you apply and meet the eligibility requirements, you may be entitled to receive the OAS pension while you are still working. To be eligible, you must be 65 or older, a Canadian citizen or legal resident, and have lived in Canada for at least 10 years after reaching the age of 18. If you live outside Canada, you may still be eligible. You must have been a Canadian citizen or legal resident at the time the pension was approved, and have lived in Canada for at least 20 years after reaching the age of 18.

HOW MUCH WILL YOU RECEIVE? In 2008, the maximum OAS payment was $502 per month or $6,024 per year. An individual who has lived in Canada for 40 years after turning 18 is eligible for the full pension. If you have lived in Canada less than 40 years after reaching age 18, you may still qualify for a full or partial pension. The OAS pension is fully adjusted for inflation and the adjustments are made in January, April, July, and October. For full details on how much pension you may be entitled to and the steps required to apply for it, contact the Federal Government office or search online under Old Age Security.

CLAWBACK: In 2008, the OAS payment is "clawed back" for recipients who have a net income of $64,718. For incomes above this level, 15 cents of each dollar is held back. For example, a pensioner who earns an additional $10,000 above the threshold income of $64,718 would have $1,500 of his OAS payment clawed back. If he earns an additional $40,185 (bringing his total income to $104,903), all of the OAS payment is clawed back ($40,185 x 15% = $6,027, the maximum OAS entitlement). Seniors in the top income tax bracket in Ontario pay 46 percent tax on each additional dollar earned. With the OAS clawed back, their total marginal tax on each dollar is really 61 percent (46 percent plus the 15 percent clawback on OAS).

Because of this clawback, it is important to pay attention to the timing of your income. If possible, delay or defer your income, take smaller amounts of money sooner, or split the income with your spouse in order to keep it below the clawback zone.

RISKS TO THE PROGRAM: OAS money is paid for out of the general revenues of the government. It is not a "funded" program, in which capital has been set aside specifically for this purpose. Over the next 50 years, with declining birth rates and an aging population, fewer workers will be supporting a growing population of retirees. Some people predict that we will see a generational revolt, with younger workers, burdened with the cost of raising a family, rebelling at the idea of paying more and more in tax to support pensions and medical services that are mostly used by seniors. However, by then seniors will make up a greater proportion of the population, and since a larger percentage of them vote compared to younger people, seniors' political power suggests that they will, at least in the foreseeable future, win the battle.

The introduction of the clawback was the first curtailment of the OAS benefit program. We suspect that any further reduction in the program will be by way of another change to the clawback provision, as opposed to a cut to the overall benefits.

## GUARANTEED INCOME SUPPLEMENT AND ALLOWANCE

**WHO IS ELIGIBLE?** The GIS provides additional income, on top of the Old Age Security benefits, to low-income seniors who live in Canada. To be eligible for the program you must be receiving the OAS and you must meet certain income requirements. The amount of GIS that a pensioner is entitled to is based on income from other sources; the higher the income from other sources, the lower the GIS. The Allowance is a similar program that is available only to individuals between the ages of 60 and 64. You must apply for both benefits.

**HOW MUCH WILL YOU RECEIVE?** The amount of the GIS depends on your marital status and the pension status of your spouse, if you have one. In 2008, the maximum monthly benefit for a single person was $634. For the spouse of a pensioner it was $419, for the spouse of a non-pensioner, $634, and for the spouse of an Allowance recipient, $410. For example, if a retired couple had an annual income from other sources (excluding the OAS) of $5,000, the GIS would be $409 per month, using 2008 rates. If their annual income from other sources was $10,000, the GIS would be $211 per month; if it was $15,000, the GIS would be $106 per month, and if it reached $20,112, the couple would no longer be eligible for the GIS. The GIS is adjusted for inflation in January, April, July, and October. To determine the exact amount you may be entitled to, contact the GIS office at 1-800-277-9914 or go to www.hrsdc.gc.ca/en/isp/oas/tabrates.

**RISKS TO THE PROGRAM:** The GIS program is funded out of general tax revenues. At some point in the future, it is possible that the program could be amended. However, as with the Old Age Security program, the political clout of seniors will likely keep the GIS in place for the foreseeable future.

## CANADA PENSION PLAN/QUEBEC PENSION PLAN

**WHO IS ELIGIBLE?** The CPP/QPP is a contributory, earnings-based pension plan. If you have worked in Canada and contributed to the plan, you are eligible for the pension. However, not every dollar of earnings is eligible for pension plan contributions. For 2007, no contributions are made on the first $3,500 of earnings. For 2008, the maximum level of earnings on which contributions can be made is $44,900. You must apply for CPP/ QPP payments.

**HOW MUCH WILL YOU RECEIVE?** The amount you receive depends on the amount you contributed. You can easily find out the amount you will be entitled to by contacting the pension office or by entering "Canada Pension Plan benefit calculation" into your web browser. The maximum amount available in 2008 was $884.58 per month ($10,615 per year). This amount is fully indexed to inflation. In addition to the regular pension benefits, a one-time death benefit of $2,500, a survivor's benefit, and a disability benefit are also available.

The pension can be split between spouses. When this happens, the total of the individual pension entitlements is added and this total is divided equally between the two spouses. When one spouse is in a higher income tax bracket than the other, pension splitting is a sensible way to reduce income tax.

**WILL YOU COLLECT CPP PAYMENTS EARLY OR LATE?** If you retire any time after age 60, you can elect to begin CPP payments. However, there is a penalty of .5 percent per month for each month your receive the pension before age 65. This means that if you begin the CPP payments at age 60, you will collect 70 percent of the full amount that would have been available if you had delayed receiving the pension until age 65.

Alternatively, if you work past age 65, you can elect to delay the start of CPP payments. This increases the pension by .5 percent for each month that it is delayed after the age of 65.

The advantage of taking an early CPP is that you can make use of the cash today. Most people who choose to take early CPP need the income. But if you didn't need the cash, you could invest it in a non-RRSP investment account. For example, Anna was entitled to the maximum CPP and took it early, at age 60. She saved every payment until age 65, earning 4 percent (after tax) on the savings. By age 65, she had built up a pool of cash in the amount of about $28,000. If she had not taken an early CPP, at age 65 she would have received about $1,000 per month, which is about $700 per month after tax. Instead, Anna receives $700 in CPP payments (which is about $500 per month after tax), plus about $93 ($28,000 x 4% = $1,120 / 12 = $93) from her "CPP savings pool." And this is while keeping her CPP savings pool intact until death. If she wanted to spend that money she could receive $150 per month in additional after-tax dollars. If she uses up her capital she will have about $715 (500 + 65 + 150) after tax.

The bottom line is that if you don't need the money, and you are able to invest wisely, it does not make much difference whether you take early CPP or not. However, it would make a big difference if you waited to collect and then died just before your 65th birthday. Had you taken it early, neither you nor your estate would benefit from the payments that would have been received.

RISKS TO THE PROGRAM: Most actuaries believe that the Canada Pension Plan is sound for the foreseeable future. The CPP operates on a "pay as you go" structure, with the contributions from current workers paying for the pensions of retired ones.

## PROVINCIAL GOVERNMENT PROGRAMS

Each province will offer a number of programs to help seniors, especially those on a low income. These programs could range from drug plans to housing assistance to tax rebates, as well as income assistance. Each province will have its own program. You can find information on provincial websites. Doing a search such as "Alberta Seniors" or "Ontario Seniors" should get you to the correct site. The resource section at the back of this book has a listing of specific websites.

### What you can do now

- Examine the CPP entitlement form you get every year and determine how much money you can expect to receive.
- If you are planning to retire before age 65, determine how much CPP you will collect.
- If you are in a lower income bracket, determine if you might be eligible to receive a GIS or Allowance.
- If you are in a higher income bracket, determine if your OAS payments will be clawed back.

- Add up what you might expect to receive from the Canadian government programs.
- Familiarize yourself with the benefit programs for your province.

## The bottom line

The various government programs—OAS, GIS/Allowance, and CPP/QPP—form a base for most people's income in retirement, and are the only source of income for many seniors. These programs are on sound financial footing and are likely to remain so for the foreseeable future. They are all indexed to inflation. Don't forget to include them in the calculation for your total income in retirement.

# Rule 13

## Make Sure You Understand Your Company Pension Plan

The company pension was once the mainstay of a retirement program and the reward for an employee's long and loyal service. Many of the parents of the people who are now getting ready to retire spent their entire working career with the same employer. It is less common for the current generation of employees to have either a full pension or a long career with one employer. In 2003, the percentage of workers who had a pension plan was 39 percent, down from 46 percent in 1991. This is a trend that is expected to continue. An important planning step for future retirees is to look into the benefits and options that exist within their employer's pension plan. The two main types of registered pension plan (RPP) are the defined benefit plan (DBP) and the defined contribution plan (DCP), which is also called a money purchase plan.

### DEFINED BENEFIT PLAN

The defined benefit plan is generally the preferred plan for employees and the most costly and most risky for employers. The "defined benefit" is usually a guaranteed pension with the amount determined according to a formula. The formula takes into consideration the number of years the employee worked with the company, the income (which is often calculated as the average of the best five years of employment), and a predetermined ratio that shows what percentage of the average income will be paid as a pension.

Because of the cost of DBPs to the employer, the number of companies that offer these plans is shrinking. Generally only public service employers and the largest corporations in the country can afford them. The trend in Canada and the U.S., has been a movement away from defined benefit plans, where the company takes the risk, to defined contribution plans, where the employee does so.

One advantage of a defined benefit plan is the reassurance of knowing that the pension is guaranteed and backed by provincial and/or federal government legislation, which ensures that the company funds the plan so that pension guarantees will be met. Another advantage is the plan's simplicity. You do not have to "manage" the investments that are generating the income you receive.

The disadvantage of the DBP is that it does not provide for any estate value. If the plan has a survivor's benefit option, your spouse will continue to collect a portion (usually 60 percent) of your pension if you predecease her. However, when you are both gone, your estate or your heirs will be out of luck.

The total benefit package to pensioners often includes both guaranteed and non-guaranteed pension benefits, such as medical and dental coverage. If you are counting on these non-guaranteed benefits, you should be aware that they can be eliminated. A recent survey by Mercer Human Resource Consulting found that, because of rising costs, 18 percent of 200 employers surveyed had reduced non-pension benefits to retired employees in the past three years and 25 percent of employers plan to take similar steps in the next three years.

## RISKS

Defined benefit plans can be underfunded. This means that actuaries have determined that more capital needs to be added to the plan to ensure that the promised pensions can be paid to pensioners for as long as they live. If a company with an underfunded plan fails, pensioners will not receive the full amount of the promised benefits. Although this does not happen frequently, it is not unheard of.

Over the past several years, much has been written about a corporate pension plan crisis. The stock market crash after the tech bubble of 1999 and 2000 and the historically low interest rates that followed have resulted in large unfunded pension liabilities—meaning that the plans do not have enough funds to pay for future pension obligations. The 2006 annual survey by the Conference Board of Canada and Watson Wyatt Worldwide found that fears about a pension plan crisis are increasing. Of the chief financial officers surveyed, 80 percent believed that there was a pension crisis, up from 59 percent two years earlier, and 61 percent thought the crisis would be long lasting. Although most pensions appear to be on a sounder footing, lingering problems could result in cutting back pension benefits, eliminating early retirement incentives, and reducing the indexation of benefits for some pensions.

## DEFINED CONTRIBUTION PLANS

The "defined" part of the defined contribution plan agreement is the amount that the employer contributes to the plan each year. After the employer meets the obligation to contribute the defined amount, usually 5 percent of the salary earned by the employee in the previous year, the employer's obligation is over. These plans are easier and cheaper for the employer to manage and administer. The obligation to make a contribution annually to an employee's plan until he or she retires is less onerous than being responsible for a pension that the employee receives for life.

With a DCP, the risk of having income for retirement lies with the employee rather than the employer. The amount of income the pensioner eventually receives depends entirely on the choices and investment decisions he or she makes as an employee. These choices include the contributions made to the plan, the asset allocation and the individual funds the employee chooses, and how well those individual funds are managed. If the employee opts for a balanced investment portfolio, the expected pension income can be conservatively estimated. If the employee opts for a higher risk/higher return asset mix, the eventual income may be either much higher or much lower.

There are two advantages to the defined contribution plan. One is that it is transferable. If you leave one company, the assets can be transferred to an RRSP. The other advantage of the DCP is that if you were to die prematurely, the balance that is in the plan can be paid (after tax) to your estate and heirs.

## RISKS

Employees are responsible for assuring that their pension assets are properly managed both while employed and when retired. However, many employees or retirees lack the skills or interest to effectively manage their pension assets. Not only do their skills fall short of professional management of a defined benefits plan, but the *costs* are higher in a DCP, and this also takes away from performance. The entire risk of assuring the DCP plan will provide enough income during retirement lies with the employee.

A weak stock market at the time you stop working or during the first few years of retirement could significantly reduce the value of your pension assets and future financial security.

## What you can do now

- Understand how your pension plan works.
- If you have a DBP, estimate your income when retired.
- Determine when you can receive full pension.
- If you have a choice between taking a lump sum or receiving a pension, do not rely solely on the advice of those who would like to invest the lump sum for you.
- If you have a DCP, estimate its future expected value when retired.
- Review the current holdings in your DCP.

## The bottom line

For those employees who still have a company or government private pension, this is the cornerstone of their retirement income. Employees who receive a monthly pension from a defined benefit plan can, for the most part, be assured that they will have a guaranteed income in retirement. Those who receive a lump sum from a defined contribution plan will have to continue to manage the assets themselves to generate income from their pension plan. In this case, "managing" the pension assets means selecting the asset mix and the individual managers who will actually buy and sell the investments.

# Rule 14

## Make the Most of Your RRSPs, RRIFs, and Personal Savings

As the number of pension plans shrinks, more retirees are relying on their own savings to provide the bulk of their retirement income. These savings are typically in either tax-deferred accounts such as an RRSP/LIRA or non-tax-deferred accounts. If, like 50 percent of all Canadians, you do not have a pension plan, you will have to rely on your own savings and your own investment management skills to provide for your retirement future.

Leading up to retirement, people are in an accumulation phase, focusing on saving money and increasing their wealth. Once retired, they enter a distribution phase, using their assets to finance their retirement lifestyle. In determining your retirement income, you must calculate how much of the income that your assets generate you will spend and how much of the capital you can draw down each year without depleting it before you die.

### RRSPS AND RRIFS

Most people understand the basic principles of RRSPs. The federal government encourages employees to save for their retirement by giving them an income tax deduction equal to the amount of the annual contribution to their RRSP. In addition to the income tax deduction, the income earned within the RRSP compounds on a tax-free basis. An RRSP does not allow the holder to avoid paying taxes, only to defer them. Taxes eventually have to be paid. For most retirees, the tax rate on the withdrawal of funds in retirement will be less than the tax they saved while working, so the net result is lower overall taxes.

By age 71, you must convert the RRSP to a Registered Retirement Income Fund (RRIF), or buy an annuity and begin to withdraw an annual income and pay the tax on the income collected. You can convert the RRSP to an RRIF at any time prior to age 71, but you cannot delay doing so beyond that age. A couple can choose to use the age of the youngest spouse for the conversion date of the RRIF. This allows for a longer deferral on the tax that will eventually be paid.

The "conversion" of the RRSP to an RRIF is not a complicated matter. The essential steps involve signing an RRIF application form, which changes the name of the account from an RRSP to an RRIF, choosing a payment schedule, and beginning to receive annual payments. The conversion to an RRIF does not require you to make any changes to the underlying investments. Presuming you had a sensibly balanced, well-diversified investment portfolio while the account was called an RRSP, you would stay in the same asset mix after the name changed to an RRIF.

The federal government sets a minimum amount that must be withdrawn each year, and you must include this amount in your taxable income for the year. In Table 4.2 below, the individual has $500,000 in an RRIF at the end of the year he turned 70. We have assumed that the RRIF will earn 6 percent a year over the course of his life. As you can see, the minimum percentage that has to be withdrawn from the RRIF increases as the individual gets older. It is only 7.38 percent at 71, but it becomes 8.75 percent at 80 and 13.62 percent at 90. When the minimum rate is greater than the rate of return, the balance left in the RRIF will go down. In this example, although the annual income is relatively stable, the amount in the RRIF drops each year and falls off rapidly after age 90.

TABLE 4.2
RRIF WITHDRAWAL ASSUMING 6% ANNUAL RETURNS
AND $500,000 AT THE END OF THE YEAR RECIPIENT TURNS 70

| Age | RRIF $ before withdrawal | Min % | Income $ | RRIF $ after withdrawal |
|---|---|---|---|---|
| 71 | $530,000 | 7.38 | $39,114 | $490,886 |
| 75 | 489,005 | 7.85 | 38,387 | 450,618 |
| 80 | 427,325 | 8.75 | 37,391 | 389,93 |
| 85 | 350,917 | 10.33 | 36,250 | 314,668 |
| 90 | 255,986 | 13.62 | 34,865 | 221,121 |
| 95 | 138,976 | 20.00 | 27,795 | 111,181 |
| Average income | | | 37,171 | |

Table 4.3 on page 101 shows how the same retiree's annual RRIF payments will vary assuming different annual rates of return. Although the withdrawal amounts are very similar at the beginning, they are quite different after 5 and 10 years. At a rate of return of 7% or 8%, the annual

payments will rise until age 90, but at the lower rates of return they will decline.

TABLE 4.3
RRIF WITHDRAWAL ASSUMING VARIOUS ANNUAL RETURNS
AND $500,000 AT THE END OF THE YEAR RECIPIENT TURNS 70

| Age | 4% | 5% | 6% | 7% | 8% |
|---|---|---|---|---|---|
| 71 | $38,376 | $38,745 | $39,114 | $39,483 | $39,852 |
| 75 | 34,900 | 36,610 | 38,387 | 40,232 | 42,148 |
| 80 | 30,906 | 34,010 | 37,391 | 41,072 | 45,076 |
| 85 | 27,241 | 31,445 | 36,250 | 41,732 | 47,981 |
| 90 | 23,820 | 28,844 | 34,865 | 42,068 | 50,670 |
| 95 | 17,265 | 21,931 | 27,795 | 35,149 | 44,352 |
| Average income | 30,730 | 33,762 | 37,171 | 41,007 | 45,327 |

Retirees who need or want the money can always withdraw more than the minimum amount; in fact, in some cases, withdrawing more than the minimum amount (or converting it to an RRIF before it is mandated) is a sensible strategy to minimize income tax. Some benefits, such as the OAS, the GIS, and the Allowance are clawed back when incomes rise beyond a certain level. In these cases, by taking an early withdrawal, the pensioner is effectively spreading the income over more years and therefore, with less income to be included each year, he or she is reducing the clawback of other income sources. In a proper tax planning strategy, the amount withdrawn would vary so as to minimize the overall tax burden and ensure that the maximum amount possible stays in the hands of the investor.

## NON-RRSP SAVINGS

All savings that have been accumulated outside tax-sheltered investment accounts form your "regular" or "cash account" savings. Non-RRSP savings can be substantial; they include, for example, the proceeds from the sale of a home or a business, an inheritance, and other savings that you did not put into RRSPs. This is also the account in which you would save any withdrawals you are required, or choose, to make out of your RRSP or RRIF, and which are not needed in order to support your lifestyle. Although it should be obvious, it is worth stating that just because you might be required, or might choose, to withdraw an amount from your registered account, does not mean you have to spend that money. If you don't need it, you should simply save it in your non-RRSP account.

Investments and income tax planning are discussed further in other sections of the book, but at this point we want to say that you should choose an asset mix that takes into account your entire investment portfolio, including your registered as well as your non-registered accounts. As a general rule, within the broad asset mix you select you should, to the greatest extent possible, hold your interest-bearing securities inside the registered accounts, where the interest will be sheltered from income tax. At the same time, hold your growth investments in your non-registered accounts, where the expected capital gains and dividends will be taxed at a lower rate.

## THE DIFFERENCE BETWEEN AN RRSP AND A NON-REGISTERED ACCOUNT

People tend to think that a dollar in an RRSP is equivalent to a dollar outside an RRSP—for example, $100,000 in an RRSP is equivalent to $100,000 in a non-RRSP account. This is far from from the truth. When you withdraw money from your RRSP/RRIF, you incur a tax expense, so in fact, the RRSP is worth only a fraction of the other account. If we assume a tax bracket of 46 percent, the $100,000 is worth only $54,000 after tax. When you are working, particularly if you are in a high tax bracket, putting money in an RRSP is always a good idea. However, once you are retired, non-registered savings accounts are preferable to RRSP/RRIF savings accounts, because the latter have a tax liability associated with them. Taxes can be deferred but will eventually have to be paid.

In Table 4.4 on page 103, the cash flow from withdrawals from an RRIF account is compared to that of a regular investment account. We assume that money coming out of the RRIF is taxed at the top rate of 46 percent and the income earned from the regular investment account is a combination of dividend, interest income, and capital gains, with an effective tax rate of 30 percent. We assume the amount withdrawn to be at the minimum RRIF rate for both RRIF accounts and non-registered accounts.

Assuming a 6 percent return, the RRIF account will generate an after-tax income of about $20,000 per year and the regular account about $30,000. The after-tax cash flow for the RRIF account will decrease year after year, while the other account will be more or less constant.

TABLE 4.4

RRIF AND CASH ACCOUNTS WITHDRAWALS

ASSUMING 6% RATE OF RETURN AND $500,000 AT AGE 70

| Age | Min. % | Amount withdrawn | RRIF after tax | Non Reg after tax |
|---|---|---|---|---|
| 71 | 7.38 | $39,114 | $21,122 | $30,114 |
| 75 | 7.85 | 38,387 | 20,729 | 30,083 |
| 80 | 8.75 | 37,391 | 20,191 | 30,134 |
| 85 | 10.33 | 36,250 | 19,575 | 30,291 |
| 90 | 13.62 | 34,865 | 18,827 | 30,518 |
| 95 | 20 | 27,795 | 15,009 | 25,435 |
| Average income | | 37,171 | 20,072 | 30,203 |

In 2009, Canadians will have a new option for saving for their retirement. The Tax-Free Savings Account (TFSA), introduced by the Federal Government in 2008, will allow Canadians to earn tax-free income in this account. In the words of a government spokesperson, "It's the single most important personal savings vehicle since the introduction of the Registered Retirement Savings Plan (RRSP)."

All Canadian residents over the age of 18 can contribute up to $5,000 per year to the TFSA. Unlike an RRSP, the contribution itself is not tax deductible. The value of the account lies in the fact that the investment income earned, whether it be from interest, dividends, or capital gains, is tax free. All investments that are eligible for RRSPs and RRIFs will be eligible for the TFSA as well.

The TFSA has a number of features that make it an attractive savings vehicle. Like RRSPs, unused contributions can be carried forward indefinitely. Also, money that is withdrawn can be put back into the TFSA at a later date without reducing the total contribution room. As an example, if you withdraw $20,000 from your TFSA, you can replace that amount at a later date. The contribution room will be indexed to inflation in multiples of $500. For example, if inflation goes up by 3 percent a year, after 10 years inflation will be 34 percent higher and the annual contribution by that time will have grown to $6,500.

For retirees, the income received from the TFSA or amounts withdrawn will not affect the eligibility of the Government Income Supplement (GIS) or the Allowance or impact the clawback of the OAS. Because of this, a TFSA might be a preferred choice over an RRSP for low-income Canadians, especially those who are approaching retirement. The benefit of reduced taxes for low-income workers is relatively small compared to the negative consequences withdrawal from an RRSP will have on Guaranteed Income Supplement (GIS) benefits.

All individuals who have no debt and who have savings in taxable accounts should contribute to a TFSA. For Canadians with conflicting priorities, such as paying down consumer debt, paying off the mortgage, and contributing to RRSPs and company pension plans, the decision to contribute to a TFSA requires more careful consideration. Nevertheless, it makes good sense to open up a TFSA even if you do not make an immediate contribution to it. When you open an account, your contribution room will be allowed to accumulate and if you have the money at a later date you will have the room to move it into the TFSA. For example, if you opened up a plan but did not make a contribution for 10 years, at the end of that period you would have over $50,000 of room to shelter a one-time windfall or extra cash that might be available, when, for example, you have paid off the mortgage.

## What you can do now

- Estimate the value of your savings and RRSP accounts during retirement.
- Determine the asset mix allocation between RRSPs and regular savings.
- Prepare an RRSP/RRIF withdrawal schedule to minimize taxes and maximize benefits of income splitting with your spouse.

## The bottom line

RRSP/RRIFs and other personal savings form the main sources of retirement income for over 50 percent of Canadians who don't have company pension plans. All accounts require proper asset management to meet income objectives with the minimum amount of risk. Because of the different tax treatment of regular and tax-deferred investment accounts, proper tax planning and allocation of investments between the accounts is required to ensure after-tax returns are maximized.

# Rule 15

## Ensure You Make the Proper Transition from Work to Leisure

What is your most valuable asset? Most people would say their house or their RRSP, maybe their business or their company's pension plan, or some other highly valued tangible asset. In fact, our greatest financial asset over our lifetime is ourselves. More precisely, it is the set of skills, aptitudes, education, experience, and wisdom that allows us to earn a living, create and run a business, and manage the wealth that we create. The ability to earn an income is an important asset that should not be ignored when planning for the future.

### WORKING A FEW MORE YEARS CAN MAKE A BIG DIFFERENCE

For many people who just can't wait to retire, the idea of working any longer than necessary is not an option. Others feel more ambivalent about working. What is certain is that working a few extra years can have a significant impact on your financial security during retirement.

In Table 4.5 on page 107, we compare Richard, who retires at 62, with David, and Maria, who work for three more years and retire at 65. Each of the three needs $30,000 per year, which can come from either savings or work, and each has $400,000 in assets. We assumed that the capital would earn 6 percent per year. In the first column, Richard's capital begins to be depleted in the first year ($400,000 x 6% = $24,000, minus $30,000 expenses = –$6,000). In the second column, David does not need to touch his capital, and in addition is able to save $10,000 on top of the $30,000 dollars he uses from income to pay for expenses ($24,000 investment income + $10,000 savings = growth of $34,000). In the third column, Maria is able to put $20,000 towards her $30,000 annual expenses ($24,000 investment income + $20,000 employment income = $44,000, less expenses of $30,000 = capital growth of $14,000).

In the first column, Richard's assets decline throughout his retirement and will eventually run out at age 90. In the second column, David's assets will actually rise every year, suggesting he could spend even more in his retirement and still be financially secure. In the last column, Maria's assets still decline, but at a slower rate than if she had quit work at 62.

Even a short period of extra income has made a big difference to her financial picture.

TABLE 4.5

RETIRING AT AGE 62 VERSUS WORKING 3 MORE YEARS

| Age | Richard age 62 | David age 65 + $40,000 | Maria age 65 + $20,000 |
|---|---|---|---|
| 63 | $394,000 | $434,000 | $414,000 |
| 64 | 387,640 | 470,040 | 428,840 |
| 65 | 380,898 | 508,242 | 444,570 |
| 70 | 340,615 | 511,030 | 425,823 |
| 75 | 286,707 | 514,761 | 400,734 |
| 80 | 214,566 | 519,753 | 367,160 |
| 85 | 118,025 | 526,434 | 322,230 |
| 90 | -11,169 | 535,375 | 262,103 |

## CHOOSING YOUR PATH TO RETIREMENT

Choosing the right path to retirement can mean the difference between a successful retirement and a disappointing one. You will almost always be better off financially by delaying your retirement, but as we've seen, financial factors are not the only things to consider. The four main paths to retirement are:

- Early retirement: Retire before 60 and give up work
- Traditional retirement: Retire between 60 and 65 and give up work
- Phased-in retirement: Retire between 50 and 60 and either work part-time or downshift to a less strenuous or more enjoyable job
- Never retire: Continue to work after age 65

## EARLY RETIREMENT

Many working Canadians dream of early retirement. The option to quit working while still reasonably young and then live a life of leisure is something many aspire to but few can afford. If you have the financial resources and are able to fill your days with meaningful activities that give purpose to your life, retiring early can be a great choice. In many cases, those who enjoy retirement the most are those who retire the earliest.

## POINTS TO CONSIDER:

- Retiring while still relatively young and healthy with complete control over your life has enormous appeal.
- Retiring early requires a greater planning and savings commitment than other retirement paths.
- People with jobs that are stressful or boring might be happier in the long run if they retire early, even though they might have to settle for a more modest lifestyle.
- Those who retire early usually give up their jobs during their peak earning years and peak saving years.
- Unless you have a company pension, retiring before 60 means you will have to rely on your own financial resources for several years before collecting either CPP or OAS.
- From a financial security point of view, giving up the best savings years of your life is a big decision and one that you must make with care.
- Retiring early also increases the time you will spend in retirement, thereby increasing your longevity risk.
- Once you retire, it may be difficult to re-enter the labour force.
- The longer you spend in retirement, the greater the danger of inflation eroding the purchasing power of capital. A pension that looked very good at age 55 might be totally inadequate 20 years later, even in the most moderate inflation rate scenario. And early retirees might live an additional 15 to 20 years after age 75.

## TRADITIONAL RETIREMENT

Most people still take the traditional path to retirement, quitting their job cold turkey between the ages of 60 and 65.

## POINTS TO CONSIDER

- Government and company entitlements and most programs are based on the traditional retirement age of 60 to 65.

- With increasing longevity, people who retire in their early 60s still have many healthy and active years ahead of them.
- By delaying retirement, people may not be able to enjoy these years fully due to poor health or an early death.
- People with physically demanding or dangerous jobs who continue to work after age 60 to 65 face increased odds of getting injured because their reflexes are slower.

## PHASED-IN RETIREMENT OR SEMI-RETIREMENT

Transitioning into retirement offers many different alternatives. It could mean keeping your existing job but working fewer hours, or downshifting to a part-time job, or taking a different job that is less stressful. Alternatively, you can phase into retirement by re-careering—beginning a new career or starting a business.

### POINTS TO CONSIDER

- For those who would like to retire early but cannot afford to do so, working part-time can be a good option. Working part-time provides structure to the week, additional income, mental stimulation, and a social network.
- Most jobs are designed to be full-time, and there may be few opportunities for part-time work with the skills that you have.
- If you want to move to a new city after retirement, the types of jobs you are qualified to do may not be available.
- Most companies do not yet have programs in place to allow for phased-in retirement.
- Once you have downshifted to a less demanding job, it will be difficult to return to your current position if you change your mind.

## NEVER RETIRE

People who continue to work past the age when most of their cohorts are retired consist of two different camps—those who have to work and those who want to. Those in the first camp are forced to work because they do not have sufficient funds to support themselves in retirement. Those in the second camp enjoy their work so much that, even though they can afford to retire, they choose to continue working.

- For most people, working will always mean a better standard of living and greater financial security than not working.
- A few more years of employment can make a dramatic difference in your financial security.
- You may be forced to retire due to poor health or a layoff.
- Many companies are currently lukewarm about keeping employees on beyond the traditional retirement age and may "encourage" workers to retire, even though mandatory retirement is abolished.
- Eventually everyone slows down and has to stop working. Individuals who do not have a balanced lifestyle and whose lives are entirely focused around their employment may not adjust well to retirement.

## What you can do now
- You can never go wrong by planning and preparing for early retirement. Once you approach that target age, you can always decide to work longer, but at least you will be prepared if you are unable to work longer or do not want to continue doing so.
- If you are considering working during retirement, either part-time or at a different job, plan well ahead of time to ensure you will have the necessary skills.
- Redo your financial plan, analyzing the impact of different working scenarios in retirement.

## The bottom line
When to retire and whether you should work during this period of your life are fundamental decisions that will impact your financial security. You should consider the different retirement paths that are available and evaluate them on a financial basis as well as a lifestyle basis. If you are relying on working in retirement, you have to consider the possibility that because of health reasons or lack of opportunities, you may not be able to.

# Rule 16

## Determine What Your Financial Assets Will Earn

What rate of return will you earn on your investments? This is a key consideration when estimating the future value of your assets and your income in retirement. One or 2 percent can make the difference between a financially successful retirement and a financially uncertain one.

As investments and savings rather than pensions become a main source of retirement income it becomes more important than ever to try to earn the best return possible on your assets. The first step should be to make a reasonable forecast of the expected average return on your investments. It is difficult to plan and budget properly without a reasonable estimate of your annual income. If you underestimate your returns you may end up working longer than you wanted to or spending less than you were able to. On the other hand, if you overestimate your returns, you may end up retiring too soon or spending too much, both of which could jeopardize your financial security.

### WHAT WILL MARKETS RETURN IN THE FUTURE?

When looking forward and trying to estimate future returns, forecasters use history as a guide. They look at past returns and assume that they will be reflected in the future. There is a natural tendency for investors and all those who advise them to extrapolate into the future what they know from their own experience. However, if retiring baby boomers assume that the market performance during the next 25 years will be similar to the last 25, they may be very disappointed.

The past 25 years was the most remarkable stretch in the history of the North American stock and bond markets. The early 1980s stands out as a period of exceptionally high interest rates, high inflation, and the worst recession since the Great Depression. The capital markets were exceptionally volatile as governments grappled with the twin evils of high inflation and high unemployment.

The fight against inflation was successful. Inflation dropped from over 12 percent in the early '80s to just over 2 percent in 2008. This allowed interest rates to fall from over 17 percent to just over the current rate of 4 percent on long-term bonds and lower on short-term Government of Canada Treasury Bills. This incredible decline in interest rates also benefited the stock market. Stocks that were trading at a P/E multiple of 8 when interest rates were high traded at 16 to 20 when they dropped. With the P/E doubling in value, stocks could double in price even if earnings did not rise.

### TABLE 4.6
### 25-YEAR PERFORMANCE TO APRIL 2007

|  | Annual Return (%) | Growth of $1,000 |
| --- | --- | --- |
| Cash | 6.87 | $5,260 |
| DEX Bond Universe | 10.74 | $12,813 |
| S&P/TSX total returns | 11.93 | $16,770 |

Sensible investors could not go wrong over most of the last 25 years. If they just held Treasury Bills during that time, their annual returns would have been 6.8 percent. Bonds returned 10.7 percent and stocks 11.93 percent. These are all exceptional numbers and above the long-term historical trends, so looking ahead it is dangerous to assume that we will see a repeat of these results. With interest rates and inflation closer to 40-year lows than they are to 40-year highs, the next 25 years, from a stock and bond market perspective, will likely be quite different from the previous quarter century. For one thing, we will not have the drop in interest rates to help propel the markets higher. Another factor is the demographic shift that is taking place. It will change the demand for financial assets in the future. Stocks and bonds are like any commodity—the greater the demand, the higher the price.

Some of the strong growth in the stock markets from the early 1980s to today can be attributed to baby boomers saving for retirement. In 1982, the average age range of the baby boomers was 18 to 36. In 2009, the range will be 45 to 63, the prime earnings and savings years. Much of the money saved has found its way into the financial markets, either directly, through RRSPs and personal savings, or indirectly, through company pension plans. Now that the Canada Pension Plan is investing in the capital markets, all workers are in fact investing money into the market, whether they have any personal savings or not. Estimates of total Canadian wealth in 2005 included $1 trillion in company pension plans, over $100 billion in CPP, $600 billion in RRSP/RRIFs, $134 billion in mutual funds, and $100 billion in stocks. Most of that money is invested in the stock market or bond market.

There is concern that an aging society, with more retired people and fewer workers, may cause downward pressure on stock and bond prices. The majority of Canadians will have to use the wealth they created during their working years to fund their retirement. In most cases, they will need to spend not only the income from the capital, but the capital as well. Their financial wealth will decline throughout retirement and most of their remaining financial assets will be sold on their death by their heirs.

Much of an individual's wealth and income comes from company and government pension plans and the Canada Pension Plan. Although the assets in these plans are still growing, many are now starting to pay out more to current retirees than is being received from those still employed. As more and more baby boomers retire and collect pensions, that trend will continue. The result? Many pension plans will be net sellers of financial assets to pay pensioners, no longer providing fresh capital to the financial markets. A few years of poor stock market returns will see this trend accelerate.

Economists worry that, as baby boomers retire, stock and bond markets could collapse as retirees sell their financial assets faster than the smaller Generation X that follows accumulates their own assets. A 2005 report, "How Global Aging Will Reduce Global Wealth," examined the impact of aging populations on wealth in Japan, the United States, and Western Europe. The authors of the report expect savings to fall dramatically in these places over the next 20 years, which could result in less demand for financial assets. As household saving rates decline, government deficits and the rising cost of health care could push interest rates higher and result in lower stock market returns.

The population of Canada grew by about 30 percent in the last 25 years, but it is expected to grow by only 20 percent in the next 25. With the baby boomers leaving the workforce over the next 20 to 25 years, the widely forecasted labour shortages might result in an economy that will not be able to grow at its full potential because many companies will not be able to find enough workers.

The net result will be a stock market that will likely not perform as well in the next 20 to 30 years as it did in the '80s and '90s. This is why it is important to use conservative numbers in your assumptions about what your investments may earn over the next 30 years.

## FUTURE EXPECTED RETURNS ON INVESTMENTS

We can only make educated guesses as to what the future returns will be. Even though we can be correct about the long-term trends, there may be extended periods of time when returns are above or below the trend line. For example, since 1955, the average total return on Canadian stocks has been 10.9 percent. However, in one 10-year period, the average return was only 3.34 percent, while in another it was over 19 percent. Similarly, in one 20-year stretch the average return was 6.22 percent, while in another it was 14.14 percent. It would make a considerable difference to your income if you started your retirement at the beginning of a 20-year period when the market future return was 14 percent versus a period that returned an average of only 6 percent. Even a year's difference in starting point can make a large difference over a 20-year period. If you had invested in the S&P/ TSX Index in June 1982, the average annual return 20 years later would have been 11.65 percent. If you had invested in June 1983, the average return two decades later would have been only 8.2 percent, well below the long-term average. Twenty years is a typical lifespan in retirement, and the average returns an investor experiences could be a function of—among other things—the year he or she retired. The difference between a very successful retirement and a mediocre one, financially speaking, could be the fact that you retired a year earlier or later.

The table on page 115 shows expected long-term returns for different asset allocations. Without going into any detail, they reflect current interest rates as of the spring of 2008, and a future stock market that will be weaker than the past 20 years due to a lessening demand for securities and high current valuations.

## TABLE 4.7
### EXPECTED LONG-TERM RETURNS FOR VARIOUS ASSET MIXES

| Type of Portfolio | T. Bill 3% | Bonds 4% | Equities 8% | Total % |
|---|---|---|---|---|
| Income balanced | $10.00 | $60.00 | $30.00 | 5.1 |
| Growth balanced | 10.00 | 35.00 | 55.00 | 6.1 |
| Aggressive growth | 10.00 | 10.00 | 80.00 | 7.1 |
| All equity | 0.00 | 0.00 | 100.00 | 8.0 |

These are educated guesses that reflect market returns. After fees, the typical investor with a balanced portfolio will likely earn somewhere between 4 and 7 percent per year over the long term.

## THE EFFECT OF TIMING OF RETURNS ON WEALTH IN RETIREMENT

It is not just the long-term average returns that impact your financial wealth, but the timing of those returns. When retirees begin withdrawing money from their investments, the returns during the first few years can have a major impact on their wealth. In the example below, the investor has $300,000 at the beginning of his retirement and takes out $30,000 every year. In each of the three examples, the average five-year rate of return is 8 percent.

## TABLE 4.8
### GROWTH OF $300,000 AT DIFFERENT RATES OF RETURN
### AND ANNUAL WITHDRAWALS OF $30,000

| | Bad First 2 yrs | | Good First 2 yrs | | Average First 2 yrs | |
|---|---|---|---|---|---|---|
| 1 | -15 % | $225,000 | 30 % | $360,000 | 8 % | $294,000 |
| 2 | -2 % | 190,500 | 20 % | 402,000 | 8 % | 287,520 |
| 3 | 13 % | 185, 265 | 13 % | 424,260 | 8 % | 280,522 |
| 4 | 20 % | 192,318 | -2 % | 385,775 | 8 % | 272,963 |
| 5 | 30 % | 220,013 | -15 % | 297,909 | 8 % | 264,800 |

At a constant 8 percent return, the investor would have $264,800 left after five years. If he started out the period with two good years, he would end up with $297,909, almost as much as he started with. However, if he started out with negative returns in the first two years, his capital would have shrunk to $220,000. Two retirees with identical wealth can have entirely different financial outcomes depending on when they start retirement. A retiree who starts out at the bottom of a bear market will have better investing success than one who starts out at a market peak.

## What you can do now

- Determine an appropriate long-term asset.
- Estimate the value of your savings into the future, using conservative estimates.
- Analyze the impact of using different rates of returns on your financial plan.

## The bottom line

Estimating the income from your investments is an important part of financial planning and preparation. Over the next 25 years, we do not expect that returns will be as rewarding as they were during the previous quarter century. This is in part due to the current low levels of interest rates and the lessening in demand for financial assets as retirees and pension plans sell their assets to finance the baby boomers' retirement.

# Rule 17

## Decide When It Makes Sense to Sell the Family Home

For many people, their home is not only their biggest asset, but also a significant source of income for retirement. A 2006 survey by RBC Financial Group found that 33 percent of those surveyed expect their home to be a source of retirement income. Of those, 40 percent said their home will account for up to half of their income in retirement. For many, converting the equity in their home into retirement income is the most significant financial decision they will make during their retirement.

The sale of the family home and the move to a different location can affect both your financial security in retirement and the overall level of satisfaction with this new phase of your life. Like many other decisions concerning retirement, the decision to sell your home should be made only after considering all the financial as well as emotional ramifications. It is important to avoid a costly "boomerang" effect—moving to a new location, then moving back to the original one because you are not happy.

### RETIRING BABY BOOMERS ARE CHANGING REAL ESTATE SUPPLY AND DEMAND

As baby boomers start to retire en masse, they could have a major impact on the price of real estate across Canada. The increase in housing prices in the 1970s was in part caused by the early wave of baby boomers purchasing their first homes. In the 2000s the increase in real estate prices, especially in resorts and desirable retirement locations, is in part due to baby boomers buying second properties to use as summer homes with the intention of retiring there.

Typically, the size of a home tends to increase as a couple ages, up until the time they retire. As couples have children and income increases, the size of the house tends to reflect the larger family and higher level of income. After children move away from home, empty nesters find themselves with more space than they need. With the loss of income in retirement, many people will not have the financial resources or physical energy to own and maintain a large, expensive house, especially if they still have a mortgage on it. As people age, the tendency for both couples and singles is to find smaller and smaller living arrangements. Many people downsize to smaller homes to free up some of the equity that is tied up in their real estate. Others do so in order to travel or for other lifestyle reasons. And for those over the age of 75, the main reason is deteriorating health.

The generation coming up behind the baby boomers is smaller, with fewer children. This will reduce the demand for the large homes that many boomers are likely to be selling, especially in urban or suburban areas. However, those areas of the country considered most desirable to live in during retirement should be in constant demand and see rising prices. That trend is already evident in "recre-retirement" hot spots. For example, in 2006, Kelowna, a city of just over 100,000 in the interior of British Columbia, with the highest proportion of seniors of any major urban area in Canada, surpassed Toronto and Victoria to become the second most expensive place to buy a home after Vancouver.

If you are counting on selling your home to fund your retirement, it is a mistake to assume that real estate prices will keep going up and that there will always be a ready market for your home. Many people who expect to sell a large house in the suburbs and buy a smaller house in a desirable retirement community might find their old home worth less than the new one they want to buy.

## SHOULD YOU SELL OR STAY PUT?

Selling the family home is always a tough decision. From a financial point of view, you want to know what impact the sale will have on your cash flow. If you downsize, will you have enough money to take more vacations or buy that recreational property? If you sell, should you rent or buy a smaller home? Will the income from investing the proceeds of the sale move you to a higher income tax bracket and cause you to be subject to the clawback?

For most people, the simplest means of converting equity from their home is to sell it and move to a rental, downsize in the same city, or move to a less expensive town or city. For those lucky enough to own property in some of the most expensive areas in Canada, the equity in their home can be significant and moving to a city or town with inexpensive housing will free up substantial capital. An extra $100,000 earning 5 percent a year can mean a big difference in a retiree's financial well-being.

The immediate financial results of selling a house are fairly easy to calculate, particularly if the sale is going to be made in the near future and the proceeds can be reasonably estimated. The longer-term impact, from lower house maintenance costs or a lower cost of living in a smaller town, are also easy to project. If you live in a large city and move to a small town or a "retirement" city such as Elliot Lake, Ontario, the savings can be significant. For example, the same quality of home that would cost $2,300 per month to rent in Toronto can be rented in Elliot Lake for $700 per month. This represents a savings of $18,000 per year. After income tax (at a marginal tax rate of 40 percent), you would need a pension of $30,000 per year to have the $18,000 additional funds to live in Toronto versus living in Elliot Lake.

You also need to consider emotional and behavioural factors when deciding whether to sell your home. Here are three different choices typical retirees have when analyzing their housing situation:

## OPTION 1: STAY IN THE EXISTING HOME
### REASONS TO STAY
- The house is conveniently close to shops, medical facilities, and activities you enjoy.
- The house is near friends and family.
- There is plenty of room for entertaining and overnight guests.
- It is set up exactly the way you want, with room for all the furniture.
- You have a strong emotional attachment to the house; it is filled with many pleasant memories.
- The house may appreciate in value and be a good investment.
- You avoid the high cost of moving, including real estate commissions and start-up costs.
- Moving can be stressful and disruptive.

### REASONS TO MOVE
- You can use the proceeds of the sale to pay off your mortgage.
- The house is far from medical and shopping facilities.
- The house and property are difficult to clean and maintain.
- The neighbourhood is changing; former neighbours are moving away.

- The house is becoming too costly to maintain.
- You could use the extra money from the sale of the house.
- Your friends and family have moved to distant parts of the country.
- Your health is deteriorating.

## OPTION 2: DOWNSIZE
### REASONS TO DOWNSIZE
- Your costs of ownership will be reduced.
- You will pay off the mortgage or put money in the bank.
- Less cleaning and maintenance will be required.
- A smaller home will be more suitable to your new lifestyle.
- You will move to a better, more convenient location.
- You will have a better quality home.
- You do not need all the space in your present home.
- A new home will allow "aging-in-place."
- It will be easier to walk away and enjoy vacations.

### REASONS NOT TO DOWNSIZE
- A smaller place may be too cramped, with no room for existing furniture or hobbies.
- You cannot find a desirable location.
- You will have less privacy in a smaller home.
- You will have less room for visiting friends and family.

## OPTION 3: MOVE TO A NEW CITY OR TOWN
### REASONS TO MOVE
- You will be closer to family and friends.
- The climate will be more to your liking.
- You will have a better quality of life.
- The cost of housing and cost of living will be lower.
- You will be closer to medical and shopping facilities.
- You will experience the adventure of starting a new life in a new location.
- You will be closer to leisure activities.

## REASONS NOT TO MOVE

- You like the town or city that you're in.
- It will be expensive to move.
- There will be fewer work opportunities at the new location.
- You are happy with the status quo.

In many instances, the home is an inseparable part of life and family history. Ultimately, however, you have to look at a home as a house. Quite simply, it is a capital asset. Whether to sell it or keep it is, in the end, a financial choice. Consider the practical financial factors. All houses need upkeep. What will it cost over the next few years in repair, maintenance, or renovation? How much additional income will you generate if you sell the house? And how much income tax will result from this additional income?

Other questions arise. Where will the money from the sale be invested? Is this the best time to sell? What gain can you expect from waiting for a better real estate market when house prices are higher? When the house is sold, what then? Where will you live, and at what rental cost? Is accommodation available in familiar surroundings near family and friends?

The following table may help you find some answers. You should also consult an experienced financial planner. Working together, you can develop the best plan for you.

### TABLE 4.9
### KEEPING OR SELLING THE FAMILY HOME

#### OPTION 1: KEEP THE HOUSE FOR ONE YEAR

|  | Sample | Your Situation |
|---|---|---|
| Net proceeds if house sold today | $300,000 | _____ |
| ADD: Increase in value during the year | $7,500 | _____ |
| (assuming home value grows at the rate of inflation) | | |
| DEDUCT: estimate for utilities, maintenance, and property tax | $8,500 | _____ |
| Net value after one year | $299,000 | _____ |

## OPTION 2: SELL THE HOUSE TODAY

| | Sample | Your Situation |
|---|---|---|
| Net proceeds if house sold today | $300,000 | _____ |
| ADD: investment income net of fees earned on net proceeds (assumed to be 5%) | $15,000 | _____ |
| DEDUCT: income tax on additional investment income (at 40%) | $6,000 | _____ |
| DEDUCT: estimated rental expense for home of similar size | $18,000 | _____ |
| Equity after one year | $291,000 | _____ |

## FACTORS, FINANCIAL AND OTHERWISE, THAT DETERMINE THE BEST TIME TO SELL YOUR HOUSE AND MOVE TO A CONDO OR RENTAL ACCOMMODATION

How important is each factor for you? Circle the number that best indicates your preference. Add up your score.

### YOUR GOALS

| | Most Important | Very Important | Somewhat Important | Not Very Important | Least Important | Your Score |
|---|---|---|---|---|---|---|
| Have no maintenance worries | 10 | 8 | 6 | 4 | 2 | _____ |
| Travel | 10 | 8 | 6 | 4 | 2 | _____ |
| Increase spending | 10 | 8 | 6 | 4 | 2 | _____ |
| Make new friends | 10 | 8 | 6 | 4 | 2 | _____ |
| Have liquid assets | 10 | 8 | 6 | 4 | 2 | _____ |
| Minimize income tax | 2 | 4 | 6 | 8 | 10 | _____ |
| Have space for family visits | 2 | 4 | 6 | 8 | 10 | _____ |
| Be protected against inflation | 2 | 4 | 6 | 8 | 10 | _____ |
| Delay lifestyle change | 2 | 4 | 6 | 8 | 10 | _____ |
| Work in garden | 2 | 4 | 6 | 8 | 10 | _____ |
| Total | | | | | | _____ |

**MORE THAN 70 POINTS:** You probably should consider selling now.

**BETWEEN 40 AND 70 POINTS:** Selling might be the easiest way to achieve your goals. You should investigate thoroughly.

**FEWER THAN 40 POINTS:** Now is not the time for you to sell.

## What you can do now

- Determine the value of your current home.
- Research other housing options.
- Estimate the total cost of moving into a different home.
- Consider the pros and cons of moving.

## The bottom line

For more and more Canadians, selling the family home is becoming part of their financial planning strategy for providing income in retirement. Those close to retirement will be able to gauge the effectiveness of downsizing to a less expensive home. However, those who might not be retiring or downsizing just yet have to consider the risk of selling during a period when a lot of other retirees are doing the same thing. Shifting demographics could change the supply/demand characteristics of the real estate market, making it more difficult for retirees to "cash out" of their home equity.

# Rule 18

## Don't Underestimate the Other Risks to Your Retirement Security

The only thing we know for sure about the future is that there will be surprises. The more distant the future, the greater the amount of uncertainty, and the more risks associated with it. As an example, the threat of high inflation in the next couple of years might be slight, but the probability of high inflation in the next 20 years goes up dramatically. While you are working, you can usually deal with financial setbacks because you have time and a steady income on your side. Once you are retired, you cannot afford to make the same mistakes.

We all face uncertainty and risks. These risks can result in unexpected costs and expenses that can jeopardize even the best-laid plans. We manage some of these risks by purchasing life insurance or health-care insurance. We can mitigate other risks by our own actions. For example, we can reduce our health risks by living a healthy lifestyle. We might set aside contingency funds to handle unforeseen emergencies. No matter how we decide to deal with these risks, it is important to understand them and consider how they might be managed. A proper financial plan takes these risks into consideration.

### DEATH OF A SPOUSE

The death of a spouse can have major financial implications that add to the grief of the surviving partner. Usually couples are financially secure while both spouses are alive and collecting two pension incomes. After the death of one spouse, income is significantly reduced while expenses—housing costs, property taxes, utilities, etc.—remain almost the same. Unfortunately, a spouse's death is often accompanied by a decline in economic status.

#### POINTS TO CONSIDER

- Grief over a spouse's terminal illness or death contributes to high rates of depression and suicide among the elderly.
- Pension income from the deceased spouse might cease or be reduced. Old Age Security and Canada Pension Plan payments for the deceased will end.

- If a partner dies in the early stages of retirement, while he or she is still earning some income from employment, that income will be lost.
- If one of the partners is disabled and the caretaker spouse dies, this may bring financial problems at the worst possible time. The surviving spouse will have to incur the additional cost of paying for care.
- If the spouse who was in charge of the financial affairs dies, the surviving partner may not be able to perform these financial duties.
- Life insurance, a proper will, and an estate plan can provide some financial protection against the death of a spouse.
- A surviving spouse usually requires about 75 percent of a couple's income to maintain the same living standard.

## CHANGE IN MARITAL STATUS

Depending on the circumstances and the individuals involved, a divorce in retirement may have a positive or negative effect on the couple's happiness. However, it will almost always have negative financial consequences. The cost of two people living apart is greater than that of two people living together. Meanwhile, the two people's combined income has not changed, in fact, and without income splitting, the total income (after tax) might even be lower. Divorce can create major financial problems for both parties, and the rate of divorce and separation among boomers and retirees is becoming higher.

### POINTS TO CONSIDER

- Marriage and divorce can change benefit entitlements under public and private plans. Make sure you understand these details before you change your marital status.
- Splitting the marital assets will almost certainly lead to an overall loss in standard of living.
- The legal and other costs involved in a divorce can erode the overall value of the assets.
- In theory, the combined income for two individuals living separately should not be less than it was when they were married, but in some cases the total after-tax income will be lower because income splitting strategies can no longer be used.

- Many retired couples who are financially secure while pensions and costs are being shared will lose this financial security if they need to maintain two households.

## UNFORESEEN NEEDS OF FAMILY MEMBERS

Many retirees find themselves helping other family members, including parents, siblings, children, or grandchildren. If these family members experience a change in health, employment, or marital status, the retiree may need to supply even greater personal or financial support.

### POINTS TO CONSIDER

- Your retirement planning should take into account any obligation or potential obligation to assist needy family members. Set up a contingency plan to cover some of the anticipated expenses.
- In addition to financial support, you may need to provide day-to-day assistance and care to family members who are sick or disabled.
- You may already know which family members may require assistance, but you should also take into account possible changes such as new marriages and grandchildren.
- Housing requirements may change if children want to return home.
- Increasingly, more and more grandparents are caring for their grandchildren.

## UNEXPECTED HEALTH-CARE COSTS

Unexpected health-care costs are likely to increase as we age. So is the likelihood of requiring day-to-day assistance. Prescription drugs can be an issue, especially for the chronically ill. Although major health-care costs are covered by the health-care system, some of the more incidental costs are not.

### POINTS TO CONSIDER

- Health changes can be sudden (if caused by an illness or an accident) or gradual (if linked to a chronic disease).
- Retirees who lose the ability to look after themselves may have to

incur additional expenses for their care or move to a costly facility.

- Consider purchasing insurance that can cover some of the unexpected health-care costs.

## CHANGES IN HOUSING NEEDS

Most people will remain in the home they lived in before retirement. However, as people age, their requirements often change. Health is one of the most common reasons seniors sell their homes. They might want to move to a residence that is wheelchair accessible or that requires less cleaning or maintenance.

### POINTS TO CONSIDER

- New forms of housing such as "independent living" and "assisted living" combine different levels of support care with housing. These types of housing can be quite expensive.
- The most appropriate form of housing for an individual in a given situation may not be available in the chosen geographic area, or may be available only after a long wait.
- A house can be a major asset that can be converted to cash by sale. But being forced to sell due to a change in housing needs can mean putting the house on the market at the worst possible time (for example, at a time when there are few buyers and prices are weak).

## STOCK MARKET RISKS

As we explained earlier, you should expect that the stock market will perform during your retirement the same way it has performed over the last 50 to 60 years. That is to say, there will be strong bull markets, when stocks generally go higher, and bear markets, when they generally go lower.

### POINTS TO CONSIDER

- A stock market correction can change people's retirement plans. Individuals losing money often adjust their lifestyles by budgeting their money more carefully, taking fewer vacations, postponing retirement, or returning to work in retirement.

- Be careful about retiring at the end of an extended bull market. Future expected returns should be lower to take into consideration the normal bull and bear market cycles.
- Diversification across different asset classes will help reduce the downside risk.

## PUBLIC POLICY RISKS

Canadians saw the impact of public policy risk on October 31, 2006. This was the date when the federal government announced changes to the rules for the taxation of income trusts. Within days of the announcement, the market value of income trusts dropped by about 10 percent. In our complex society, much of our life and our financial security is governed by public policy. We have no way of knowing what circumstances might develop that could force the government of the day to change the rules in any number of areas.

## POINTS TO CONSIDER:

- All levels of government—municipal, provincial, and federal—can make changes that can have a major impact on retirees. For example, the government could change the eligibility rules for OAS or the GIS, or it could alter CPP benefits.
- Some Canadians are at risk of public policy change by foreign governments. For example, the U.S. government could change tariff and duties on Canadian goods, which could have a negative impact on some Canadian industries and towns.
- Public policy changes that affect seniors as a group will likely be mostly positive at least for the next few years.

## HOUSING MARKET RISKS

Many people see equity in their home as a source of income in retirement. However, as with other assets, you cannot assume they will keep on rising. Witness what has happened to the housing market in the U.S. in 2007/2008, when prices dropped across the country and in some areas declines were over 20 percent, with a record number of foreclosures.

### POINTS TO CONSIDER

- Housing is foremost a local rather than a national market. A town that is suffering due to a weak local economy and a declining population will not experience a strong demand for housing no matter how much prices are going up across Canada.
- At any given time, even the owners of very fine homes might have difficulty finding willing buyers.
- Housing is not a liquid market, and homes can remain unsold for months.

### EMPLOYMENT RISKS

Losing your job before you retire can obviously have a major negative impact on your plans. You may intend to work during retirement in order to supplement your income, but there is no guarantee you will be able to do so.

### POINTS TO CONSIDER

- You may be forced to quit work due to deteriorating health or because you have to take care of a spouse or other family member.
- You may be forced out of work because of a poor economy or because your employer is failing or restructuring.
- Your current job skills may no longer be in demand.
- There may not be any opportunities to work in the area you live in or wish to move to.
- If you start a new business, it might turn out to be less successful than you hoped, and it might even fail.

### What you can do now

- Be conservative when estimating your future income and expenses.
- Understand and consider all risks when making your retirement plans.
- Risks will change from year to year. Update your financial plans periodically to reflect the current risks.
- Consider purchasing insurance to protect you against certain types of risks.

## The bottom line

We all face uncertainty and risks in our lives. These risks can result in unexpected costs and expenses that can jeopardize even the best-laid plans. It is always a good idea to have a plan B to fall back on if plan A has gone off the rails. A proper financial plan takes these risks into consideration.

# Part 5

## Follow a Simple and Sensible
## Investment Process

COMPUTERS, THE INTERNET, AND GLOBALIZATION HAVE TRANSFORMED THE WORLD OF INVESTING for the individual investor. Dedicated TV channels broadcast news about the economy and stocks 24/7. Individual investors now have information at their fingertips that previously would have been available to only the largest banks, brokerage firms, and their wealthiest clients. The currency of investing is not money but information, and information is now a commodity that is available to everyone. Small investors who used to trade their stocks through middlemen or brokers can now do so directly. With a few keystrokes and a couple of mouse clicks, individual investors can trade stocks instantaneously for pennies a share.

With the mutualization of stock and bond markets, investors can now go down to their local bank branch and buy mutual funds as easily as depositing a cheque or opening up an account. The mutual fund companies and professional managers in charge of the funds do not just manage money; they also "manufacture" products. Like companies that make soap, they have "wholesalers" who distribute their products and advisors who then sell them to their customers. The companies want to sell you their products and grab as large a share in this profitable business as possible. All the banks, insurance companies, mutual fund companies, and investment dealers are fighting for customers, and the battleground is your wallet.

The financial market has now gone beyond the plain vanilla mutual funds that allow an investor to buy a small piece of the stock or bond market. The complexity and the quantity of investment products now make it difficult for the average investor to choose wisely. In many cases, those providing the advice are also finding these products difficult to understand. But there is one thing you can be sure of—those who manufacture and manage these new investment products understand them fully, far more than the unsuspecting client who buys them. In economics, there is a term for this—asymmetric information. Asymmetric information exists when sellers know much more about a product or a service than buyers. For example, used car salesmen have more information about a specific car than the individual who is considering buying it. Research has shown that when sellers know more than buyers, the result is often that an unsophisticated buyer pays more for a product than it is really worth. And the more complex the product, the more an unsophisticated buyer is willing to pay for it.

The good news is that financial innovators have also created some very simple and inexpensive products. The creation of investment products such as exchange traded funds (ETFs) and low-fee index mutual funds can offer wide and inexpensive diversification. When you look at the fees charged by full service brokerage firms or the total cost of buying actively managed mutual funds, it is hard to believe that these low-cost alternatives exist. One reason the fees have remained high is that the average investor still believes brokerage firms and high management expense ratio (MER) mutual funds are necessary in order to manage her money wisely. This is a view that the industry would like to perpetuate for as long as possible. Another reason is the fact that many people "buy" investments without fully understanding what they are buying or all the costs associated with the products.

The investing landscape has changed in another significant way. From the bottom of the bear market in 1982 up until 2007, we have seen a remarkable, unprecedented bull market. Looking forward to the next 25 years, however, many of the same factors responsible for higher stock market returns will not be in place and the upward trend may reverse itself. Interest rates, now close to 40-year lows, are not likely to retreat further, and over the longer term the only direction they can go is higher. Over the next 25 years the investing landscape will be different and nobody knows how it will play out, but one thing that almost everyone agrees on is that future returns on the stock and bond markets will be lower than in the past 25 years.

Many investors who are contemplating retirement today gained most of their investing experience since 1982. An individual who turns 60 in 2009 was only 33 in 1982. Many of those who are currently in the industry, including strategists, research analysts, and portfolio managers, have worked exclusively during this extraordinary market. "Experienced" advisors who provide investment advice are even younger. A "veteran" advisor who is 40 in 2009 was only 13 years old at the bottom of the bear market in 1982. The result of living and working during an unprecedented bull market is that many potential retirees, and those who advise them, have expectations that are shaped by results that are better than long-term averages.

While you are working, it makes sense to shoot for a higher return, even if it increases the probability of a serious loss. In retirement, you don't have the time to recover from a serious loss and the impact can be significant to your lifestyle and financial security. You should take no more risk than is necessary to ensure that you can continue your lifestyle without ever running out of money.

While you are working, you have some inflation protection, but in retirement your investments must provide protection against inflation. An extended period of high inflation can do as much to destroy the purchasing power of your assets as a bad bear market. It is crucial to ensure your assets are protected from the ravages of inflation. In retirement, your investing goal should not be simply to provide consistent and predictable income, but also to protect your capital from inflation. It is a delicate balancing act, but the set of principles laid out in this section will help you create a long-term investment plan and ensure your investing success.

# Rule 19

## Focus on the Investment Process, Not the Products

How do you become a successful investor? If everyone has the same universe of stocks, bonds, and mutual funds to choose from and if no one can consistently predict how the markets will move, why are some investors more successful than others?

The financial services industry, dominated by the big banks, insurance companies, and mutual fund companies, aggressively sells investment products to the public. Because of this, many investors believe that the key to financial success is to find the best investment product, whether it is a hot new issue, a mutual fund that has recently enjoyed exceptional performance, a well-researched stock idea, or a new "structured" product with guarantees. We believe, however, that the key to successful investing is not to find the best new *product,* but to follow an investing *process.*

Following an investing plan or process does not guarantee success at all times, but it greatly improves the odds of being successful. This is a principle well understood by all experienced and successful investors. An investment process establishes the rules and outlines the steps you take. It gives you control over those things you can control. For example, you cannot control what your investment will do, but you can control the level of risk you will take. You might not be able to always pick winners, but you can improve your chances by having a disciplined investment strategy. Your investment portfolio might not always outperform the market, but you can make it less complicated and easier to manage to help improve your odds of doing well. You can choose to pay less in fees, allowing your investments to return more of their performance to you.

### What you can do now
- Think about your overall investment objectives.
- Analyze the steps you currently take to achieve those goals.
- Ask yourself what guiding principles you use to make investment decisions.
- Ask yourself how confident you are in your current investment program.

- Consider getting an unbiased second opinion on your investment portfolio.

## The bottom line

In the end, successful investing is not about buying those stocks or mutual funds that you think will do well. It is about having an investment process in place that will improve your odds of doing well. It is not about investment *products*; it is about an investment *process*.

# Rule 20
## Take No More Risk than Is Necessary

In a well-designed investment portfolio, higher returns are associated with higher risk and prudent investors take no more risk than is necessary to achieve their financial goals. If you can achieve all of your goals (including your estate ones) with an average return of 6 percent, then aim for 6 percent. Don't aim for an average return of 8 percent, because the higher return target requires additional risk, and the downside of additional risk is the possibility that someday you will lose so much of your capital that it will have a negative effect on your lifestyle.

To follow this principle, there are two steps you must take. The first is to prepare a financial plan that shows the rate of return that you need to achieve your financial goals. This sets your investment objectives. The second is to determine the appropriate asset mix based on the rate of return requirement. The allocation of your investments among the different asset classes, such as cash, equity, bonds, and global investments, is the cornerstone of your investment plan. The goal is to allocate assets to each class so that you achieve your required rate of return with the lowest amount of risk.

Why is this common sense principle not followed? One reason is that most investors do not know what rate of return they require to meet their goals. This problem can be easily solved by having a financial plan prepared by a competent and unbiased advisor or financial planner. Another reason is that many investors do not know what asset mix they have, never mind what would be an appropriate one. It is very common, especially for mutual fund investors, to have a poor understanding of their overall asset mix. With mutual funds, particularly balanced funds, it is difficult to know what you really own.

Many investors take more risks than are prudent or appropriate because of a very common human emotion—greed. Even if they already have enough, they ask themselves, "Why not go for the higher return?" We have enjoyed such a long period of friendly markets that most people who are retired or planning for retirement have forgotten (or have never experienced) a serious bear market. Certainly the unprecedented bull markets of 1982 to 2007 have rewarded investors who took risks.

As well, the financial services industry encourages investors to take more risks than necessary. Those in the industry are paid more when investors take more risk. Take a look at the MERs, or management expense ratios, on Canadian mutual funds. The table below shows the average MERs for some representative mutual fund asset classes. The classes are arranged with the lowest risk investments at the top and the highest at the bottom. The fees paid on the higher risk equity investments are 61 percent higher than those paid on the lower risk bond investments. The ability to earn higher fees on riskier investments puts the financial industry in a conflict of interest.

### TABLE 5.1
### AVERAGE MERS ON DIFFERENT ASSET CLASSES OF MUTUAL FUNDS

| Asset class | MER (%) |
| --- | --- |
| Money market | 1.08 |
| Short-term bond | 1.69 |
| Canadian bond | 1.73 |
| High-yield bond | 2.19 |
| Canadian balanced | 2.47 |
| Canadian equity | 2.79 |
| Emerging market | 2.83 |

Source: Globefund.com, February 28, 2007

Many people still work with an advisor who provides them with investment advice and executes their trades, whether it is for stocks, bonds, or mutual funds. The majority of investment advisors are hard-working, competent, and have their clients' best interests at heart. However, they do not get compensated based on the quality of the advice they give, but rather on the level of revenue their clients generate. Many times, the goals of the client and the objectives of the advisor are not aligned and there is a potential for a conflict of interest.

As a general rule, when your account grows larger, your financial advisor makes more money. It is also true that over very long periods of time equity investments produce a higher average rate of return and are more volatile than fixed-income investments. So one of the best ways for your advisor to increase her income is to have your capital grow. In theory, there is nothing wrong with your advisor wanting you to do well. The problem is reflected in the question "Who takes the risk?" In the typical account, the client takes all the risk of a market downturn. It is your capital and lifestyle that will be affected if you take too much risk and incur greater than necessary losses. The advisor loses an account, but you lose your life savings.

Riskier and more volatile investments help the industry in other ways as well. Typically, the riskier the securities, the more volatile the portfolio will be. A more volatile portfolio requires a more "active" style of management. More active management translates into more commissions for those providing the advice.

The industry has cleverly devised a method for determining the appropriate asset mix. It plays on our naturally greedy nature and generally supports the bias towards equities. The method is the use of the risk tolerance questionnaire. In theory, by asking questions about how you feel about risk and how you will react when your portfolio is down by a certain percentage, the advisor can determine your tolerance for risk and put you into the right investment portfolio. The advisor will try to find out how much pain you can bear before you panic and sell. If the risk tolerance questionnaire determines that you can take a loss of 30 percent before you panic, the portfolio will be designed to be as aggressive as possible without exceeding this pain threshold. In effect, the portfolio is set up so that it is almost certain that someday you will experience the maximum amount of pain that you say you can bear. Of course this is all nonsense. When people panic they no longer think rationally, so any attempt to predict how they will react when they desperately fear they are going to lose everything is a waste of time. Also, clients are notoriously bad at estimating their tolerance for risk. When everything is going well, they have a high tolerance for it. But after only slight losses that extend over several months, everything changes and their tolerance levels drop to zero.

### What you can do now

- Determine the rate of return required to meet your long-term financial objectives.
- Determine the realistic returns your existing portfolio and investment strategy are expected to generate over the long term.
- Rethink your current objectives, investment strategy, or expectations if there are differences between the two steps above.

### The bottom line

In the end, investing is not about trying to shoot the lights out. It is not about trying to make as much money as you can without any regard for risk. Smart investing is about trying to meet your financial goals. If you can meet your financial goals with little risk, then all the better. This is especially true for those in retirement. If you don't have a job that can help overcome losses caused by investing mistakes, you are prudent to take no more risk than necessary.

# Rule 21

## Understand How Much Your Portfolio Might Fall in a Bear Market

Many investors would not take the chances they do if they understood the potential downside risks associated with their investment portfolio. Overestimating downside risk happens less frequently than underestimating it, but some investors do make this mistake. If you take too little risk, you may have too little protection against the risk of inflation and income tax and may not earn enough income to maintain your lifestyle.

Although well-diversified portfolios will eventually bounce back after falling in value, investors face three problems with unexpected losses. First, it may take a long time to recover from a serious loss. (It takes a 100-percent return to recover a 50-percent loss.) Second, the fear of further losses causes many investors to sell just when the portfolio is at its lowest point. Third, at the bottom of a bear market the buying opportunities are the best, but those who suffered large losses will not have the money or the confidence to buy at this time. If your holdings are concentrated in a few securities or a hot sector—for example, technology in 2000—the loss you experience could be far more serious than the overall market loss, and you might never recover from it.

There are several reasons why investors often underestimate the amount by which their portfolio could fall. The main reason is that they do not have a good understanding of their actual asset mix. They may think they are in a portfolio with 50 percent equities and 50 percent fixed income, but in fact the split is 70 percent equities and 30 percent fixed income. Investors also tend to underestimate the amount by which the average stock will drop in a severe bear market. They think the average drop is about 10 percent when in fact it is closer to 30 percent. At the top of a bull market, just before the start of a bear market, many investors have a portfolio of risky stocks that will fall off considerably more than the average ones. Finally, many investors think in terms of percentages rather than real dollars. If you have an investment portfolio of $400,000, the idea of a 25-percent drop may not be too scary, but a potential loss of $100,000 seems much worse.

## How Not to React in a Bear Market

It is a fact that equity investments will occasionally drop 20, 30, 40 percent or more. In situations where the client begins in an investment portfolio that is too aggressive at the start of a bear market, the financial advisor's efforts to help may make matters worse. After the first leg down in the bear market, the shocked client has lost about 10 percent and will consider selling equities. The financial advisor will trot out all of the old arguments about why you should not sell or reduce equity exposure—you're in for the long term; markets always go up in the long run; Warren Buffett didn't sell in the last downturn; now is the time to buy, not to sell; stocks always bounce back. More than likely the advisor will be successful and the worried investor will decide to hold onto all of his positions.

The first leg down is usually followed by a rally and the advisor will take full credit for her wisdom in keeping her client invested. In the next leg down the client may be down by about 20 percent and the advisor will have to work harder to keep him invested. Since the advisor is a good salesperson and has established some level of trust, she will probably again talk the client out of the idea of selling equities. The second leg down will be followed by another leg up and once again the advisor will be able to say "I told you so."

In the next leg down the client may be down by about 30 percent and this time the advisor's words are to no avail. The client has panicked; the fact that many newspaper articles say that things may get worse is the last straw. He insists on selling some or all of the equities. It is the capitulation of the retail investor that defines the bottom of a bear market. If the average investor has not capitulated, it simply means that the market has not yet reached bottom.

So what has the financial advisor really accomplished? By allowing the investor to be in a portfolio that was riskier than necessary and then by convincing him not to sell at the first occasion when the losses were minimal, she has multiplied his actual losses.

There is a saying in the industry that "In a bear market, he who panics first panics best." In other words, when you are in a bear market, unless your portfolio is designed to protect, you don't want to be the last one to bail out.

## What you can do now

- Calculate how much you would expect your portfolio to fall if the overall market dropped by 20 to 30 percent.
- Estimate the downside risk for each major position in your portfolio.
- Determine the factors that will negatively impact your portfolio.

## The bottom line

Many investors are oblivious to the downside risk and look only at the upside potential when making investment decisions. With all their attention focused on upside potential, they wind up taking more risk than necessary. It is important to understand the downside risk and to ensure that the risk of your portfolio is appropriate for you. If you are in the correct asset mix at the start of a bear market there is no need to take any action except to rebalance your portfolio annually to keep with the plan. However, if you are taking more risk than necessary at the beginning of a bear market, you should reconsider your asset mix as soon as possible.

# Rule 22

## Diversify Your Investments, but Don't Overdiversify

Some people think a stock market crash is just around the corner and will occur as soon as they are fully invested. They think of 1929 and can imagine being totally wiped out if they invest in the stock market. It is true that you could lose a significant amount of your capital if you are 100-percent invested in stocks, but sensible investors do not put all of their eggs in one basket. If you are in a diversified portfolio and have only 40 percent in stocks, the most you are likely to lose is 20 percent of your entire portfolio. A loss of this magnitude would be a disappointment, but over a long retirement, the risk of inflation and income tax is a more serious threat to your financial security.

As a general rule, the more asset classes and the larger the differences among them, the greater the diversification and the lower the risk to the portfolio as a whole. Similarly, within an asset class (such as Canadian stocks), the greater the diversification by sector and management style, the lower the risk. Within an asset class, risk is reduced by investing in securities that have low or negative correlation to each other. For example, if you buy an oil stock and an airline stock, the loss on the airline stock—when the price of oil increases—will be offset by the gain on the oil stock.

Investing internationally provides diversification that you cannot achieve by limiting your portfolio to Canadian equities. The Canadian stock market is poorly diversified with a narrow industrial focus. As of January 2008, in Canada, over 75 percent of the S&P/TSX was made up of financial, energy, and material stocks. As a general rule, in an equity portfolio, broad geographic diversification reduces volatility (risk) and increases the average rate of return by taking advantage of investment opportunities outside Canada. Canada now represents just over 3 percent of global capital markets and investing globally reduces risk by exposing investors to a more diverse group of companies and industries. Investing internationally also gives protection against a drop in the Canadian dollar.

To ensure a diversified portfolio, you need to invest in different asset classes. If the entire equity component of your portfolio is invested in six Canadian banks, you are not diversified. If your entire portfolio consists of 10 Canadian equity mutual funds, you do not have a well diversified portfolio; in fact, you will be overdiversified in Canadian equities.

It is natural for investors to have a "home country bias" because they are more familiar with the companies that operate domestically. Favourable income tax rules on dividends paid by Canadian corporations make it seem logical to "overweight" Canada rather than to aim for 3 percent exposure to Canadian equities. In most cases, a rule of thumb would be to split the equity portion of the portfolio so that approximately 50 percent is in Canada and the other 50 percent is outside.

The traditional asset classes are stocks, bonds, and cash, and a well-balanced and properly diversified portfolio will include all three. Additional diversification, and therefore reduced risk, can be expected when small amounts of other asset classes, such as precious metals, commodities, REITs (Real Estate Investment Trusts), emerging markets, hedge funds, and high-yield bonds, are also included as part of the mix.

Investors who have a portfolio made up of individual stocks and bonds are often underdiversified or over-concentrated in one type of stock or investment. They might have over 50 percent of their portfolio in energy stocks, or too many income trusts, or mostly bank stocks. A stock portfolio can be properly diversified with as few as 20 or 30 stocks if they are well chosen, but fewer than 20 normally means the portfolio is underdiversified.

Some mutual fund investors mistakenly believe that if one fund is good, 10 must be better. Their problem is overdiversification or "diworsification," as some call it. Investors often create this problem by investing in a number of different mutual funds that have similar investment strategies within the same grouping of shares. In a portfolio with too many similar mutual funds, the good ones are offset by the bad ones and the possibility of outperforming the market is significantly reduced, if not negated.

An investor who owns five mutual funds that all invest in Canadian stocks will likely be overdiversified. In the Canadian equity market, the net result is a portfolio that will match the overall market before fees. But because of the high management fees the end result will be that the portfolio will underperform the overall market by the amount of the fees. An investor who owns a single ETF that represents the underlying market will almost always outperform the investor who is overdiversified with too many mutual funds in that same market.

## What you can do now

- Determine your current asset mix. What is the allocation among stocks, bonds, and cash?
- Ask yourself whether this current mix is appropriate for your objectives.
- Analyze your current portfolio. Ask yourself whether it is over-concentrated or over-diversified.
- If necessary, determine the steps you must take to properly diversify your portfolio.

## The bottom line

Investment management is both an art and a science. Picking stocks or mutual funds might be considered an art, but diversification—building a portfolio that is designed to meet your objectives with the minimal amount of risk—is the science of investing.

# Rule 23
## Follow an Investment Strategy

The most common reason why investors fail to reach their objectives or become dissatisfied with their portfolio performance is the lack of an overall investment strategy. Institutional investors always have a well-articulated strategy that keeps them focused and disciplined. They monitor their performance constantly; they are on top of the markets and their investments. They are constantly adjusting their portfolio to reflect both a changing investment environment and their client's objectives. When they make changes to the portfolio, they do so after careful thought to ensure the new investment fits within the overall mandate for the portfolio. With a well-established strategy, the professional money manager can remain disciplined and act rationally, even when the markets are in turmoil.

In the world of investing there is a long-standing debate about the merits of an active management strategy versus a passive investing one. Not surprisingly, major investment dealers, banks, insurance companies, mutual fund companies, and active money managers, all of whom reap huge profits from active management, support this strategy. Academic research, on the other hand, tends to support passive investing.

Active managers believe that they can add value to a portfolio by picking securities that will, on average, outperform the market. To do this, they use literally hundreds of methods, including technical, fundamental, and economic analysis. Active management is the predominant form of money management today and most mutual funds are considered to be actively managed. Because this strategy involves higher management fees, managers not only have to outperform the market—they also have to outperform it after fees and costs are deducted.

Passive investment management assumes that it is very difficult to outperform the market. Rather than try to "beat the market," managers match it and do so as cheaply as possible. This strategy is called passive investing because managers do not make decisions about which securities to buy and sell. They simply mirror the index. Since the advent of index mutual funds and exchange traded funds, individual investors can now buy broad sectors of the market. The advantage of passive management is that it is much less expensive to manage investments and the cost savings are passed on to the investors. For example, the ETF for S&P/TSX 60 Composite Index has a cost of 0.17 percent per year versus 2.79 percent for the average Canadian equity mutual fund. On a $100,000 investment, this would mean management fees of $170 per year for the ETF, versus $2,790 for the mutual fund.

## ASSET MIX ALLOCATION AND SECURITY SELECTION

When investing, you must also decide what the asset allocation of your overall portfolio should be (what asset classes will be used and what percent of the portfolio will be in each asset class) and what securities belong in each asset class. For each decision, you can take either an active or a passive approach.

**PASSIVE ASSET ALLOCATION/PASSIVE SECURITY SELECTION:** This is the simplest of all strategies. An investor picks a long-term or strategic asset mix that is appropriate for his financial goals and risk tolerance. The asset mix is rebalanced occasionally to ensure that the long-term asset allocation is maintained. Index funds or ETFs are purchased to represent the underlying asset classes. This strategy suits investors who are not interested in the day-to-day monitoring of the markets and who feel they are unable to add value to either asset mix or security selection.

**ACTIVE ASSET ALLOCATION/PASSIVE SECURITY SELECTION:** In this strategy, investors adjust their asset mix depending on their overall views of the markets. If they believe that stocks are going to outperform in the short term, then they might overweight the equity asset class in their portfolio. Another name for active asset allocation is tactical asset allocation. As with passive asset allocation/passive security selection, index funds or ETFs are purchased to represent the underlying asset classes. This strategy might be appropriate for investors who take a top-down approach to investing in the market but have little interest or skill in security selection. A top-down approach is one in which the investor believes that global or macro trends will impact the markets in a certain way. For example, an investor might fear that a recession is looming and elect to reduce exposure to equities.

**PASSIVE ASSET ALLOCATION/ACTIVE SECURITY SELECTION:** Investors who use this strategy pick a long-term or strategic asset mix that is rebalanced occasionally to ensure that the long-term asset allocation is maintained. For each asset class, individual securities are purchased in the belief that the investors will outperform the stock market using their skills in stock selection. These investors have little interest or skill in tactical asset allocation.

**ACTIVE ASSET ALLOCATION/ACTIVE SECURITY SELECTION:** In this strategy, investors adjust their asset mix depending on their overall views of the markets. If they believe that stocks are going to outperform in the short term, they might overweight the equity asset class in their portfolio. For each asset class, they purchase individual securities with the belief that they will beat the market. This strategy may be appropriate for those investors who take a top-down approach when they are investing in the market and who also believe they have superior stock-picking skills.

## COMBINING ACTIVE AND PASSIVE STRATEGIES

Many investors combine active and passive strategies within their portfolio. For example, they might buy individual securities for the Canadian part of their portfolio and then purchase ETFs for exposure to the U.S. and global stock markets. Alternatively, they might combine an active and passive strategy within one asset class. For example, an investor might have 50 percent of her Canadian portfolio in an ETF and 50 percent in individual securities. This approach is called "core and explore," or the core/satellite approach.

### What you can do now

- In three or four sentences, state your current investment strategy. If you cannot state your strategy, then you do not have one.
- Evaluate your current investment skill and ability realistically.
- Determine which part of your portfolio should be passively managed and which part should be actively managed.

## The bottom line

One of the things that separates the professional money manager from the typical individual investor is that the professional has a disciplined investment strategy and the individual usually does not. A well thought-out strategy provides the investor with a set of rules and guidelines that help to focus on the task at hand and remove emotions from the investing process.

# Rule 24
## Keep Your Investment Portfolio Simple

A well-diversified and simple portfolio is usually better than an over-diversified and complicated one. This is especially true for the individual investor who does not have the time, analytical tools, or expertise to manage a complex portfolio properly. Many of today's mutual fund investors have portfolios that are extremely complicated, making them difficult to understand, monitor, or alter as the market environment changes. It is not uncommon for some mutual fund investors to have an overall portfolio with a level of complexity that might rival that of a pension plan worth billions of dollars.

With a simple portfolio, you can make investment decisions more easily and with more confidence as the capital markets evolve or your personal circumstances and objectives require a change in the asset mix. If your portfolio is too complicated to see what you own, you will find it difficult to know if or when you should make an adjustment. For example, if you decide to put 10 percent of your portfolio in U.S. investments, you may not know whether the appropriate change is to reduce your exposure to the U.S. or to increase it.

Why do investors get into portfolios that are too complicated to manage? One reason is the lack of experience and understanding on the part of the investors and those who advise them. Investors hold the misguided belief that the more mutual funds and other investments they have, the better diversified they are. In many cases, the resulting diversification makes the portfolio worse, the performance deteriorates, and the portfolio becomes more complicated, not better.

Another reason for complicated portfolios is that many advisors are more concerned about not doing significantly worse than the market than they are about trying to outperform it. Adding more and more funds will make it less likely that they will significantly underperform the market in any one year. But it will also almost guarantee that the portfolio will never outperform because of high fees. It is much simpler and cheaper to buy an ETF representing an underlying benchmark than it is to buy a number of mutual funds, each trying to outperform that same benchmark.

The final reason for complicated portfolios is the reluctance, on the part of both advisor and client, to recognize mistakes. As long as the mistake is still in the account there is always the hope that it will bounce back. There is a natural tendency in the industry to make buy recommendations more quickly than sell recommendations. New investment products are becoming available all the time and it is tempting to persuade clients to purchase a hot new product rather than add to one of the existing positions in the portfolio.

A simple portfolio of half a dozen well-selected mutual funds, index funds, or exchange traded funds will tend to do better over the long run than an excessively complex portfolio that contains 20 or 30 mutual funds. It is also easier to administer and understand.

### What you can do now

- Analyze your current investment portfolio. Is it easy to understand and manage?
- Do you know how your portfolio is presently allocated among the different asset classes? If the answer is no, your portfolio is too complicated.
- Do you understand each position you are holding and the reason for owning it?
- Examine the ways you could simplify your portfolio while keeping it properly diversified. A good first step would be to sell the securities that are an insignificant part of your overall portfolio.

### The bottom line

In investing—as well as in many other human endeavors—the acronym KISS (keep it simple, stupid) is appropriate. A well-diversified but simple portfolio is preferable to a complex and overdiversified one. Not only is it easier to manage, administer, and understand, but it is also likely to outperform one that is more complex.

# Rule 25
## Know What Rate of Return You're Earning

It is essential for you to know the rate of return you earn on your investments. You cannot manage your portfolio effectively or monitor the performance of your financial advisor without this information.

If you pay close attention to the rates of return that you earn on your investments, you will be able to determine which investment strategies work (and why), and whether you are on track to meet your long-term goals. You can adjust strategies that don't seem to be working or add funds to those that appear to be successful. Proper performance measurement can help you determine whether certain investments should be retained or replaced. If you are working with an advisor and your investments are consistently doing poorly, you may decide to fire the advisor. If you are managing your own money and getting poor returns, you may choose to "fire yourself" and hire a professional.

### What you can do now
- Analyze the performance of the mutual funds and other securities in your portfolio.
- Go to www.showmethereturn.ca to calculate the return of your portfolio as a whole.

### The bottom line
People who regularly monitor the performance of their investments generally do better.

# Rule 26

## Compare Your Investment Returns against a Proper Benchmark

In addition to knowing the percentage rate of return you're earning, you need to have a benchmark or reference point that will allow you to determine if the actual return is acceptable. In the investing world, a benchmark is a standard against which you can compare the performance of a stock or portfolio. The most widely known benchmark is the Dow Jones Industrial Index. You need two benchmarks in order to manage your capital wisely, an absolute and a relative one.

### ABSOLUTE BENCHMARK

The first benchmark is your personal absolute return. Let's say your financial plan has indicated that you need a return of 7 percent to be able to achieve your financial goals. You need to determine if you are earning, on average, at least 7 percent. If your investment portfolio returned an average of 4 percent per annum over the last five years, then it is not meeting the rate of return you require. You will either have to change your asset mix to a more aggressive one or modify your financial goals.

This information, although helpful, does not in itself show what action you should take to get your portfolio on track to achieve your long-term goals. It does not show how well you managed your portfolio or whether you need to change your investment strategy. The low rate of return may have been a reflection of a poor stock market over the last five years; a strong recovery in the market may bring the performance back on target. The rate of return may also have resulted from a bad decision in setting the asset mix, or from poor money management. You need more information, and a relative benchmark, to decide what to do to get your portfolio back on track.

### RELATIVE BENCHMARK

A relative benchmark tells you the performance of your investment portfolio compared to a market index. For example, let's assume that you bought a mutual fund that was invested in Canadian stocks. Over the past five years, the mutual fund showed an annual return of 8 percent. Was that fund a good choice among all the others that you could have purchased?

Did the fund manager do a good job in adding "value"? If, over the same period of time, the most commonly used performance benchmark in Canada, the S&P/TSX Composite Index, returned 10 percent per year, the mutual fund clearly underperformed by 2 percent. The fund manager did not add value because you could have invested in the benchmark through an index fund or an exchange traded fund and almost matched the performance of the benchmark.

A relative benchmark helps investors decide whether to keep or sell funds. Without this reference point, an investor may not know that a fund is underperforming and may delay taking corrective action for several years. It is very important to know how performance compares against both an absolute and a relative benchmark.

## INVESTMENT BENCHMARKS FOR CANADIAN INVESTORS

Canadian investors have several different benchmarks they can use depending on what they want to measure and which asset class they want to compare. Rather than using an absolute benchmark of, say, 7 percent, many large pension plan managers use a benchmark relative to the rate of inflation—for example, the rate of inflation as measured by the consumer price index (CPI) plus 4 percent. If the average rate of inflation was 2.5 percent over five years, the benchmark over that period would be 6.5 percent. Over the long term, protecting the purchasing power of the investment is very important, so having a relative benchmark based on inflation is often appropriate.

Some of the common benchmarks for the different asset classes are shown in Table 5.2 below:

TABLE 5.2
BENCHMARKS FOR DIFFERENT ASSET CLASSES OF MUTUAL FUNDS

| Asset class | Benchmark |
| --- | --- |
| Cash | Scotia Capital 91-Day T-bill Return Index |
| Fixed income | DEX Bond Universe Total Return |
| Canadian equities | S&P/TSX Composite Total Return Index |
| U.S. equities | S&P500 Composite Total Return Index in Canadian $ |
| Equities for rest of world | MSCI EAFE Total Return Index in Canadian $ |

## USING PERFORMANCE BENCHMARKS

Using benchmarks to monitor investment performance fundamentally changes an investment strategy. Designing a portfolio without a benchmark as a reference point becomes strictly an exercise in stock picking. An investor does not know if she is in fact doing a good job of picking stocks, or if the stocks are going up because the overall market is rising. However, with the goal of outperforming the benchmark, the investor's portfolio is in effect competing against the benchmark's portfolio. As in sports, the more you scout the other team, understand its strengths and weaknesses, the style of play, and who the stars are, the more prepared you are to develop a strategy to beat it.

If you have a Canadian stock portfolio, for example, and your benchmark is the S&P/TSX 60 Composite Index, then your team, or portfolio, is up against the 60 players or stocks of the index. As well as picking good stocks and knowing how to weight them in your portfolio, understanding the composition of the benchmark will help you outperform the index. When trying to beat the benchmark, it is just as important to know what to leave out of the portfolio as what to put in it. In 2001 and 2002, when Nortel was a large component of the S&P/TSX Index and the company was collapsing, the decision to underweight Nortel relative to the S&P/TSX Index meant the difference between outperforming the index and underperforming it. Those investors with a well-diversified portfolio that did not contain Nortel would have easily outperformed the market.

Using performance benchmarks also provides a different perspective on risk. The most common way of measuring risk is in absolute terms—the volatility of the portfolio or the downside risk. When investors measure performance against benchmarks, another measure of risk becomes important. Tracking error or active risk is the risk of the portfolio performance deviating from the benchmark. The more the portfolio differs from the benchmark, the riskier the portfolio becomes. An investor can now choose to develop a portfolio with little active risk—one that performs like the benchmark—or develop one with significant tracking error. An ETF or an index fund, for example, that is meant to duplicate a specific benchmark, has negligible active risk relative to that benchmark. Investors who manage portfolios that look very similar to or mimic a particular benchmark are called closet indexers. However, a portfolio containing only a few of a benchmark's stocks will have a large tracking error relative to that benchmark.

Most professional investors will use a benchmark against which to measure performance and most of them will have a good understanding of the benchmark they are trying to beat. With a benchmark as a target, the investor can have one of two objectives. One objective is to invest in securities with a goal to beat the benchmark. Another is to invest in securities that will have less risk than the benchmark. Using a defined benchmark simplifies the investing decisions because there is a specific target to aim for. When trying to outperform the benchmark, the securities you leave out of the portfolio are as important as the ones you put in.

### What you can do now

- Determine a benchmark for each asset class.
- Choose an appropriate composite benchmark to measure your portfolio performance against.
- If you do not know how you've done compared to the appropriate benchmark, go to www.showmethebenchmark.ca and calculate your performance.

### The bottom line

In the process of managing money wisely, measuring the performance of an investment portfolio and comparing it against a benchmark are two of the most important actions you can take. They help to determine if your investment plan or strategy is on track and allow you to take corrective action before it is too late. It is impossible to manage your money wisely if you do not compare your results with a benchmark. Do not make the mistake of believing that you don't have to review performance because your advisor is looking after it—what you are really doing in this instance is measuring the performance of your advisor. And it is not fair to ask her to evaluate her performance—only you can do that.

# Rule 27

## Pay No More in Fees and Commissions than Is Necessary

As an investor, you cannot control interest rates or the stock market, but you can control the amount of fees you pay. Fees and commissions are a necessary part of buying investment products, services, and advice. The concern is not how much you pay in fees but what value you receive in return. If you use a discount broker, pay minimal fees, and your portfolio consistently underperforms by 3 or 4 percent per year, are you better off than the investor who pays 1.5% in fees and whose portfolio consistently outperforms by 3 or 4 percent year? Of course not.

The impact of fees on performance is significant. For example, a portfolio of $100,000 in mutual funds with an average MER of 2.5 percent will mean $2,500 per year in management fees. For the average investor, over a lifetime of investing, a small difference in fees paid can really add up. In Table 5.3 below the investor starts out with $100,000, contributes $5,000 a year, and earns 8 percent annually. Even though he is paying only a 2 percent fee per year, he ends up with 33 percent less after 25 years than if he had been paying no fees at all.

### TABLE 5.3
### IMPACT OF FEES ON NET WEALTH

Fee comparison assuming $100,000 initial investment, $5,000 per year additions, and 8% annual returns

| Years | No fee | 1% Fee | 2% Fee |
|---|---|---|---|
| 5 | $176,266 | $169,009 | $162,008 |
| 10 | 288,325 | 265,797 | 244,989 |
| 15 | 452,977 | 401,548 | 356,036 |
| 20 | 694,906 | 591,946 | 504,642 |
| 25 | 1,050,377 | 858,988 | 703,510 |

Investing can be easy and cheap. You can buy 1,000 shares of each of the 20 biggest and best companies in Canada, and the total cost in commissions can be as low as $200 at some online brokerage firms. If you own these shares for 20 years, you will never pay an annual fee. As a shareholder, you will receive regular reports and the dividends owed you. If you wanted to buy shares in 60 of Canada's biggest and best companies, you can do that cheaply as well with the purchase of an exchange traded fund. The iShares S&P/TSX 60 allows investors to buy a security that will duplicate the underlying index. An investor buying 5,000 shares of the iShares S&P/TSX 60 for $400,000 would pay a commission of $50. The annual cost would be 0.17 percent, which works out to $680.00 per year.

Although investing can be cheap, advice is sometimes expensive. Buying mutual funds from a financial advisor/mutual fund salesperson with that same $400,000 will be more costly. A front-end load or a sales charge of 2 percent would be $8,000 and annual MER fees of 2.5 percent would be an additional $10,000. The investor's total first-year cost is $18,000, which pays for the advice of the advisor and the cost of managing the assets in each mutual fund. If the result of the advice is consistent outperformance of the investor's portfolio, then the fees are justified and the investor is receiving excellent value for the cost. On the other hand, if the performance is consistently poor, then the investor is receiving poor value for the cost.

Fees and commissions paid for professional advice and the management of your investments are your cost of doing business, and for those on the other side of the transaction, business is very good. Your goal as an investor is to ensure that you receive good value for the fees you pay. That is no different from buying any other product or service. However, to ascertain if in fact you have received good value, it is important to understand the fees, commissions, and hidden charges that you pay.

## COMMISSIONS AND SALES CHARGES

These are by far the easiest fees to understand and the most transparent. They are the fees you pay for buying and selling securities and they are added to the total cost of your transaction. If you buy 1,000 shares at $40 per share from a full-service investment dealer, the total commissions might range from $400 to $800 depending on the firm and the advisor. Of course it does not cost that much to do the trade itself; you can do it online for $10 to $30 at an online discount brokerage firm. The $400 to $800 in commission pays for the personal service, advice, and research that the firm and advisor provide. Since brokerage fees were deregulated over 20 years ago, fees are negotiable, and as a client you should try to negotiate the best commission rate you can.

Mutual funds have three types of sales commissions: front-end load, deferred sales charge (DSC) or rear-end load, and no-load. With a front-end load, the client pays a commission at the time of purchase. It can range from 1 to 5 percent. With a deferred sales charge, the buyer does not pay any commission up front, but he will pay a fee if the units are sold before a certain time elapses (typically seven years). Buying DSC funds is generally not recommended because investors often make bad investment decisions. They feel locked in and may avoid redeeming a poorly performing fund because of the charges that will be incurred. No-load funds are those that have no sales commission attached. Typically these funds have to be bought directly from a mutual fund company.

The mutual funds sold by the major banks generally have no commissions associated with them if you buy them at the branch, nor do the mutual funds you buy online at a discount brokerage firm. Some advisors will waive the fee on a front-end-load fund. Like brokerage fees on stocks, the front-end loads on mutual funds are negotiable. In theory, just about all mutual funds are no-load, if you can find someone to sell them who will waive the commission.

## SPREAD TRADES

These types of securities are bought directly from an investment firm or bank rather than using the firm as a broker to buy from another investor who is selling the security on the market. Spread trades are common in bonds, currencies, and new issues. For example, assume you want to buy a corporate bond. The price on the firm's bond desk might be "101 bid and offered at 102." This means you can buy it from the bond desk at $102, but if you sell it to them, they will only pay $101 per $100 face value. A retail client wants to buy $10,000 dollars face value worth of the corporate bond. The advisor might charge $1.00 per $100 face value. So the cost to the investor of the $10,000 face value is actually $10,300. If the client wants to sell the same bond the next day, assuming the same price and $1.00 commission, he will in fact get only $10,000. The cost of making the trade does not show up as a commission or sales charge, but it will impact the client's overall performance just the same.

Currency transactions are the ones most people forget about. Those investors who actively trade U.S. securities in a Canadian dollar account or RRSP have to be careful about the cost of the currency exchange. Let's assume that at your investment firm the bid/ask on the U.S. dollar is $1.0025/$1.0175. This means that if you buy $1 U.S. it will cost you $1.0175 Canadian but if you sell $1 U.S you will be paid only $1.0025 Canadian. Let's assume that you sold a stock of a U.S. company in your RRSP and after commission you received $40,000 U.S. Your account would be credited with 1.0025 x $40,000, which equals $40,100 in Canadian dollars. The next day you wanted to use the $40,100 to buy a U.S. stock. After conversion, the $40,100 ($40,100/1.0175) would equal $39,410 U.S. Just converting back and forth cost you $590 U.S. People who frequently trade U.S. dollar securities in their RRSP or Canadian cash account can end up spending a lot of money in foreign currency conversions. For those who have some flexibility, with investments outside an RRSP it is always better to invest in U.S. securities in a U.S. dollar account.

### MANAGEMENT FEES

Many products and services available to investors have management fees attached. These include wrap accounts, fee-only accounts, discretionary managed accounts, accounts with investment counselors, closed-end funds, exchange traded funds, and mutual funds. Although each managed product and service has a different fee structure, we will focus on the costs of owning mutual funds, the most popular retirement investment vehicle.

Fund management fees not only pay for the portfolio manager to look after the portfolio; they also pay for the GST, the expenses of communicating with unit holders, and trading costs. The MER is equal to the total expenses divided by the total value of the fund. It is expressed as a percentage and is a good estimate of what it costs the mutual fund investor per year for the management of the fund. Mutual fund MERs typically vary between 1 and 3 percent and are deducted from the fund on a monthly basis.

Mutual fund management fees are what we would call "stealth" fees; the mutual fund companies know they are there, but they are not picked up on the radar of the typical mutual fund investor. They are completely hidden from view. As an investor, you do not receive an invoice for the fees, nor is there any itemized accounting telling you how much you paid. They are quietly deducted from the overall fund with no fanfare, just a consistent regularity. You would have to go to the company website fund prospectus, or another supplier of mutual fund data to find an estimate of what the fees are. Mutual fund fees can add up and they do impact performance. Assume an investor started with $100,000 and invested an additional $5,000 per year in mutual funds that have an average MER of 2.5 percent. If the investment returned 9.5 percent per year before fees were deducted, then after 25 years the investor would have over $810,000. During this period he would have paid over $240,000 in fees.

Fees are a hot topic among the commentators and critics of the mutual fund industry in Canada; they believe that the fees might be excessive. And, in fact, a recent academic study published in a paper called "Mutual Fund Fees Around the World" found that Canada is the country with the highest mutual fund fees.

Hidden in the MER for most mutual funds is a trailer fee, which is an ongoing commission paid by the fund company to advisors and dealers for ongoing service and advice. Typically the trailer fee is about 1 percent per year. So if you have $100,000 in mutual funds, your advisor and the company she works for will earn about $1,000 per year to provide "advice and service." Since you are paying for it, you should ensure that you are in fact getting good "advice" and good "service." Investors who buy their mutual funds at a discount broker still pay the trailer fee. It goes to the discount broker, even though by regulation these companies cannot give you advice, and the service they provide is minimal.

### INDEX-PROTECTED NOTES AND OTHER GUARANTEES
Investors can buy a number of products that have a principal protection guarantee. Examples are index-protected notes, segregated funds, and

## Wrapped Up in Fees

Erich had about $650,000 in a mutual fund wrap account at a large Canadian financial institution. The account contained mutual funds that were combined to meet his investment objectives—a balance between income and growth. It was a well-constructed portfolio, and although the fees, at 2.5 percent, seemed high, they were competitive with similar wrap accounts. However, hidden deep in the prospectus was an item about fund expenses. It said that the individual funds would have an additional 0.4 percent in fees paid annually for expenses the fund would incur, and these fees would be charged to the funds themselves. After GST of 6 percent on the 2.5 percent was added to the fund expenses, the actual total fees Erich paid directly and indirectly were closer to 3.05 percent, not the 2.5 percent advertised.

Erich had just over 50 percent, or $325,000, of the portfolio in fixed-income investments. Over the past year, the benchmark for fixed-income investment returns was 3.9 percent, and given the current low interest rates, returns of 4 to 5 percent per year was all that he might expect to earn in the near future. So, if we assume that his fixed-income investment before fees earned 4 percent, the total amount earned on his investment of $325,000 would have been $13,000. However, after estimated fees of $9,900, his return was only $3,100. Between the advisor, the brokerage firm, and the mutual fund companies, Erich paid fees over three times the amount he earned from his fixed-income investments.

other products that have an insurance component. The rule of thumb is that the more guarantees, the greater the protection, and the more complex the product, the greater the fees associated with it. If an investment product is too complicated to understand, it often means there are some hidden costs and features that make it less desirable than it appears in the glossy brochure.

## FEES IN A LOW-RETURN ENVIRONMENT

If your portfolio is going up by 20 percent per year, you may not be too concerned about fees, but in the future the returns from the stock market are expected to be in the 6 to 8 percent range. If your mutual fund earns 8 percent before fees, your 2.5 percent MER now represents over 30 percent of your total gross return. If you earn 5 percent before fees, the annual fees will represent 50 percent of your gross return, and if your fund's gross return is 2.5 percent, the fee eats up 100 percent of the return and you make nothing. When you invest in mutual funds that are consistently outperforming the stock market, you are receiving good value and the fees are well earned. On the other hand, when your mutual funds are consistently underperforming, any fee is excessive.

A number of alternatives exist for those who seek lower fees. One solution for investors with $500,000 or more is to go with an investment counsellor firm. Another choice is to use low-fee mutual funds. These are generally not recommended by financial advisors because the funds do not pay trailer fees. The third option is to buy low-cost ETFs.

### What you can do now

- Estimate what you have paid in management fees and commissions over the last year.
- Determine the number as a percentage of total assets.
- Decide whether you have received good value and service for the fees you paid.
- If you are planning to work with a new advisor, always negotiate the fees before you move your account, because this is the time when you have the most leverage.

## The bottom line

Fees and commissions are a cost of investing. If you receive good advice, excellent service, and fair performance, the fees are justified. If you receive bad advice, second-rate service, and poor performance, the fees are too high no matter how much you paid. If you are not getting good value for the fees you pay, it may be time to rethink your current investment plan.

# Rule 28

## Optimize the Location of Your Assets to Minimize Your Tax

Canadians do not have many ways to reduce the taxes they pay on their employment income, other than contributing to an RRSP. However, when income comes from investments or withdrawals from an RRSP/RRIF, they have greater flexibility.

Most investors can save more than they expect by following an income tax awareness strategy. In this section, you will learn about the allocation of different types of assets between tax-deferred accounts (RRSP/RRIFs, for example) and taxable accounts. This strategy can have a pronounced effect on income tax once a retired investor starts to draw down assets. This is due to the fundamental differences between RRSP/RRIFs and taxable accounts.

Although you can grow your RRSP tax free, eventually you will have to pay taxes as you withdraw the money to finance your retirement. In retirement you have to remember that the RRSP/RRIF now has a large income tax liability associated with it. Withdrawals are taxed as regular income, regardless of whether the withdrawal came from the original amounts contributed, accumulated interest income, accumulated dividends, or capital gains. By contrast, you pay no tax when you add money to or take money out of a taxable or "open" account. However, you do have to pay income tax on a yearly basis on the income earned in a taxable account. In this type of account, interest, dividends from Canadian corporations, capital gains, and capital losses are all treated differently by the Canada Revenue Agency. Interest income is taxed at the full marginal tax rate, capital gains and dividends get preferential treatment, and realized capital losses can offset capital gains.

Investors who have money in RRSP/RRIF accounts as well as taxable accounts can benefit by allocating their assets between the different accounts. The taxable account would contain the higher-risk securities, including the ones that pay dividends from Canadian corporations. The RRSP/RRIF would hold the lower-risk interest-bearing investments. Without changing the overall asset mix of your portfolio as a whole, the correct allocation of the investments between the different accounts can save thousands of dollars in tax over the course of your retirement.

For example, let's suppose you are starting to take money out of your RRIF. Assume you are in a 40 percent tax bracket and realize a $30,000 capital gain that year and then withdraw the same $30,000. You will pay tax of $30,000 x .40 = $12,000. If that capital gain is in your taxable account, you will pay tax on only half of the capital gain—$15,000 x .40 = $6,000.

## ALLOCATING ASSETS PROPERLY BETWEEN ACCOUNTS

At age 70, Alan has $300,000 split evenly between his RRSP and cash account. Starting at age 71, he begins taking out $15,000 from each account, for a total of $30,000 per year to finance his retirement. He is a "balanced" investor with an average tolerance for risk and his investment portfolio is 50 percent Canadian equities and 50 percent fixed-income investments. He makes 8 percent on equity investments and 4 percent on his fixed-income investments. If we assume each account is balanced with 50 percent equities and 50 percent fixed income, Alan will run out of money at age 86. In his cash account, he will have paid total taxes of $25,800, and on his RRIF withdrawals, $96,000, for a total tax bill of $121,800. After tax, he will have received $214,000 from his cash account and $144,000 from his RRIF, for a total amount of $358,000.

However, let's assume nothing else changes except that Alan now has 100 percent of his equities in his cash account and 100 percent of the fixed income in his RRIF account. The overall asset mix remains the same, a 50/50 balance between equities and fixed income. In his RRIF he runs out of money at age 84, but he does not run out of money in his cash account until age 91. In his cash account he has paid $32,000 in taxes but only $84,000 on the RRIF withdrawals, for total taxes paid of $116,000—$5,000 less than in the first example. After tax he will have received $282,000 from his cash account and $126,000 from his RRIF, for a total after-tax amount of $408,000. That is $50,000 more than in the first example! Even though the overall asset mix remained the same and the returns were the same, by putting 100 percent of the equity in the cash account and 100 percent of the fixed income in the RRIF account, Alan ends up with $50,000 more after tax than if the assets had been split evenly between the two accounts.

TABLE 5.4
## ALLOCATING ASSETS BETWEEN ACCOUNTS PROPERLY

|  | Scenario #1 | Scenario #2 |
| --- | --- | --- |
| **PORTFOLIO SUMMARY** | | |
| Total portfolio asset allocation | $300,000 | $300,000 |
| Equities | 50% | 50% |
| Fixed income | 50% | 50% |
| Yearly withdrawal | $30,000 | $30,000 |
|  | | |
| **ACCOUNT BREAKDOWN** | | |
| Money in RRSP | $150,000 | $150,000 |
| Amount invested in stocks | $75,000 | $0 |
| Amount invested in bonds | $75,000 | $150,000 |
|  | | |
| Money in open account | $150,000 | $150,000 |
| Amount invested in stocks | $75,000 | $150,000 |
| Amount invested in bonds | $75,000 | $0 |
|  | | |
| Total amount invested in stocks | $150,000 | $150,000 |
| Total amount invested in bonds | $150,000 | $150,000 |
|  | | |
| **RESULTS** | | |
| Money received from open account | $214,000 | $282,000 |
| Money received from RRIF | $144,000 | $126,000 |
|  | | |
| Total payments received | $358,000 | $408,000 |
| Total taxes paid | $121,800 | $116,000 |
| Taxes paid on open account | $25,800 | $32,000 |
| Taxes paid on RRIF withdrawals | $96,000 | $84,000 |
|  | | |
| Investor runs out of money | Age 86 | Age 91 |

## What you can do now

- If you have financial assets in both RRSP/RRIFs and taxable accounts you should allocate the investments properly between the two types of accounts.
- Place your interest-bearing investments inside a sheltered account (RRSP, RRIF, LIRA, or LIFF) and your capital-gains producing investments in an "open" or taxable account.
- Consider how to withdraw funds from an RRIF in order to minimize the tax impact.
- Ask your financial advisor for a tax-efficient allocation of your investment asset.

## The bottom line

Most retirees would have more money to spend on themselves and more to leave for their heirs if they paid attention to minimizing income tax, or more correctly, maximizing after-tax returns.

# Part 6

## Construct a
## Solid Investment Portfolio

AS AN INVESTOR, YOU HAVE THREE OPTIONS WHEN YOU ARE CONSTRUCTING AN INVESTMENT portfolio: building it from the stocks and bonds that make up the capital markets, using mutual funds or other managed funds, or using some combination of the two. With any of these approaches, you can develop an investment portfolio that will meet your investment objectives, be well diversified, and perform well. Building a sensible portfolio is not that difficult to do, but you need to understand the strengths and limitations of each option to be successful. This also holds true when investors start to use their accumulated wealth to provide income in retirement. Products that you would never have considered in the accumulation phase—for example, annuities and reverse mortgages—might make sense as a retiree, but you should consider them only after doing the necessary research.

# Rule 29
## Know the Strengths and Weaknesses of Mutual Funds

For many people, investing in mutual funds is not only their preferred choice—it may be their only choice. This is the case for those who have group RRSPs or defined contribution plans. Also, for investors with limited amounts of capital, mutual funds may be the only choice if their goal is a diversified investment portfolio. Investors should be aware of the advantages and disadvantages of mutual funds. Although these funds are professionally managed, you still need to ensure that the overall portfolio is properly constructed and diversified.

Up until the early 1980s, mutual funds were an afterthought in the Canadian investment landscape. Investors would mostly buy individual stocks and bonds or Guaranteed Investment Certificates (GICs), or leave the money at the bank in a savings account. In the middle of the 1980s, the mutual fund market exploded. In 1985, there was just $10.7 billion invested in mutual funds in Canada. By January 2008, just over 20 years later, the amount had grown to $735 billion, roughly $23,000 for every resident in Canada. It is safe to say that mutual funds are the investment of choice for most Canadians today.

Obviously, the mutual fund industry is a big business. According to the Mutual Fund Dealers Association of Canada, over 68,000 salespeople are registered to sell mutual funds in Canada. That number does not include those working at investment dealers, who can sell stocks and bonds as well as mutual funds. If we conservatively assume that the average MER is 2 percent, then the industry will generate about $15 billion a year in revenue from fees alone!

### ADVANTAGES OF INVESTING IN MUTUAL FUNDS
PROFESSIONAL MANAGEMENT: This is perhaps the main advantage of owning a mutual fund. An investor has access to professional management for his assets. The manager is responsible for selecting the best securities to meet the objectives of the fund and to outperform their benchmark.

**DIVERSIFICATION:** A mutual fund can provide excellent diversification, much better than would be possible with individual stocks and bonds. A portfolio can be invested in 60 to 100 or more securities across many countries and industrial sectors. Because the funds of many investors are pooled, there are economies of scale regarding trading costs and other fund costs. The larger the mutual fund, the greater the economies of scale. Theoretically, these savings should be passed on to the mutual fund holders in the form of lower fees.

**VARIETY OF FUNDS:** Investors can choose from many different types of mutual funds. Some invest in particular asset classes including money markets, bonds, income trusts, Canadian stocks, global stocks, and real estate. Others invest in Canada or globally. There are even funds of funds. The downside of the myriad of funds is that choosing the correct one becomes more difficult.

## DISADVANTAGES OF INVESTING IN MUTUAL FUNDS
**COSTS:** It costs money to buy and manage mutual funds. Many critics say these costs are too high.

**PROFESSIONAL MANAGEMENT IS NOT INFALLIBLE:** Since mutual funds essentially represent the overall market, at any given time 50 percent will have performed better than the average fund in their class and 50 percent will have performed more poorly. Also, mutual funds cannot protect you from overall market weakness. If you own mutual funds that contain mostly Canadian stocks and the Canadian market drops, your funds will fall in value as well, no matter how skilled or lucky the professional fund manager is.

## TAX COMPLICATIONS
Buying and selling within a fund creates a series of taxable transactions. Capital gains will be triggered and the fund holder will have to pay a capital gains tax.

Distributions of capital gains are typically done at year end and can pose a problem for investors who bought the fund near the end of the year. They will have to pay a tax on capital gains that were realized throughout the year even though they could not have benefited from the appreciation. Similarly, investors who buy a mutual fund with large unrealized capital gains on the securities in it will have to pay a capital gains tax when those securities are sold. This could add additional tax liabilities for those investors who bought mutual funds at the tail end of a bull market. It is quite conceivable that if a market is falling and the investor's mutual fund goes down in value, but securities in the fund are sold realizing capital gains, the fund holder will be paying capital gains tax on distributions from the fund—even though it is losing its value.

## CHALLENGES FACED BY MUTUAL FUND BUYERS

All mutual fund buyers face two main challenges. The first is knowing what they really own and ensuring that the portfolio is well balanced, properly diversified, yet not over-diversified. The second is overcoming the obstacle of high fees, which are a constant drag on a portfolio's performance.

Choosing mutual funds likely to outperform the market is difficult. Today, with over 2,000 mutual funds in Canada, the mutual funds are the market! It is as unrealistic to believe that most mutual fund managers will be able to beat the market as it is to believe that most students in a Grade 9 math class will get better than average marks.

### TABLE 6.1
### MEDIAN CANADIAN MUTUAL FUND PERFORMANCE, FEBRUARY 2007

| Years | Cdn. bonds | | | Cdn. stocks | | | Cdn. balanced | | |
|---|---|---|---|---|---|---|---|---|---|
| | % | Index | Diff. | % | Index | Diff. | % | Index | Diff. |
| 1 | 3.8 | 5.36 | -1.56 | 12 | 14.43 | -2.43 | 8.6 | 10.66 | -2.06 |
| 3 | 3.6 | 5.37 | -1.77 | 14.4 | 16.41 | -2.01 | 7.5 | 11.5 | -4.00 |
| 5 | 4.7 | 6.68 | -1.98 | 11.1 | 13.5 | -2.40 | 6.3 | 10.49 | -4.19 |
| 10 | 5.1 | 6.86 | -1.76 | 8.5 | 9.68 | -1.18 | 6.4 | 8.47 | -2.07 |

Source: Globefund.com

Benchmarks: DEX Bond Universe Index, S&P/TSX Composite Index and 60% S&P/TSX Composite Index and 40% DEX Bond Universe Index

Countless studies have documented the performance of mutual funds. These studies show that on average, more than 50 percent will underperform the underlying market. Table 6.1 above shows the average performance of different classes of Canadian mutual funds and compares them against their appropriate benchmark. For example, the average performance of a Canadian equity fund was 11.1 percent per year over a five-year period ending February 2007. The overall Canadian market as measured by the S&P/TSX Composite Total Return Index was 13.5 percent over the same period. The three categories of mutual funds listed all underperformed by a minimum of 1 percent over the different periods. We would expect similar results for different classes of mutual funds.

## TIPS FOR BUYING MUTUAL FUNDS

When purchasing a mutual fund, as when buying any other product, you need to make an informed choice. Ask yourself: What type of fund do I want (equity, fixed income, foreign, Canadian)? How does the fund complement the overall portfolio? (It is the overall portfolio that is important, not the individual parts.) And last, will the fund I pick do better than most of the others in the same class? Obviously, no one wants to buy a fund that will do worse than average. Choosing a fund that will show superior performance is a key consideration. Here again it is unrealistic to expect that your financial advisor can consistently pick funds that will provide superior performance in the future.

When purchasing a mutual fund, you need to understand what you are buying and why. What is the investment mandate? Is it a balanced fund or an equity fund? Is it Canadian or global? What is the fund's investment philosophy and strategy? What has to happen in order for the fund to outperform its peers? For example, a Canadian equity fund that is overweighted in energy stocks will probably outperform its peers if oil prices rise.

It is important to buy a fund not only on its own merits, but also based on how it will fit into the overall portfolio. Will it help to reduce risk or enhance performance? Does it complement other funds? Does it fill a gap in the overall portfolio or is it replacing a fund that you believe will do poorly?

Don't forget to "look under the hood." What is the current asset mix? What is the industrial sector and geographical composition? You can't judge a book by its cover, and you can't buy a mutual fund by its name only.

# Mutual Fund Mumbo Jumbo

Dave and Sheila had over $750,000 invested in mutual funds spread over 11 different accounts with three different advisors. They had over 80 different positions using 42 different mutual funds. Their largest position was $33,000 in a global equity fund, and they had 15 different positions with less than $5,000 in each. They were invested in funds of all shapes and sizes, from Canadian to global, from fixed-income to equity, from resource-based to technology-based. They had 15 funds that predominantly invested in Canadian equity and another 15 that were balanced. Some were front-end loaded and others had deferred sales charges.

We asked the couple three simple questions: Do you know what the asset mix is overall? If you needed some money, do you know which funds to redeem? Do you know your investment strategy? The answer to all our questions was "No." On further analysis, we found that 29 of the 42 funds had underperformed their respective benchmarks the previous year and, combined, they had underperformed by $17,480 or about 2.3 percent. This was only slightly less than the average MER of 2.46 percent that we estimated Dave and Sheila had paid in fees the previous year. The funds had underperformed by about the same amount as the fees the couple had paid.

The problem is not that the portfolio as a whole underperformed by 2.3 percent last year, but that it is almost guaranteed to always underperform by that much. During a 30-year retirement, this underperformance will amount to hundreds of thousands of dollars of hard-earned money that is wasted in active management fees.

For example, CI Signature Select Canadian Fund, according to its name and mandate, is supposed to invest primarily in Canadian stocks. However, as of February 28, 2007, only 48.7 percent of the fund was invested in Canadian securities. AGF Canadian High Yield Bond Fund's mandate was to invest primarily in Canadian fixed-income securities, but it had only 49.9 percent of its investment in Canada. And Trimark Canadian Small Companies Fund's mandate was to invest mainly in Canadian companies, but only 57.9 percent of its investment was in Canada.

Investing doesn't need to be complicated. If you don't understand a particular investment product or mutual fund, don't buy it. There are plenty of others to choose from.

### LESS IS OFTEN MORE

One of the biggest mistakes investors make is believing that adding mutual funds will spread the risk around and improve their chances of doing well. A good mutual fund portfolio can consist of just one fund, as long as it is a good, global-balanced fund, consisting of an appropriate mix of bonds, Canadian equities, and foreign stocks. There are few good reasons to own more than 6 to 10 good-quality mutual funds—five core mutual funds to invest in the main asset classes such as cash, fixed income, Canadian equity, U.S. equity, global equity, and more specialized funds that might be added to help improve overall diversification and performance. These could include high-yield funds, precious metal funds, emerging markets, and small-cap funds.

### KEEP IT SIMPLE

A portfolio of mutual funds should be easy to understand. You should know the overall asset mix and understand what each fund invests in. As the market changes, it is important to understand the portfolio so that you can make intelligent investment decisions about which funds to buy, switch, or redeem.

A good, balanced fund, especially one that is balanced internationally, would be a good choice if you were to own just one or two funds. It may seem paradoxical, but a portfolio containing 6 to 10 balanced funds seldom makes a good investment; it merely adds complexity, neither reducing risk nor enhancing performance. When building a portfolio containing more than three or four mutual funds, you should purchase only funds that are "pure"—i.e., funds that invest in only one asset class. For example, you might have one fund that invests strictly in Canadian equities, another that invests in fixed income, and another that invests in U.S. stocks. This way, you will be able to determine your asset mix at a glance. If you want to make a change to the mix, you can do so much more easily than if you owned many balanced funds, each invested across different asset classes.

## UNDERSTAND ALL FEES AND COMMISSIONS

Mutual funds is a big and profitable business for both those who "manufacture" funds and those who "distribute" them. It is important to understand all the fees you pay, because these costs directly reduce your portfolio's performance, dollar for dollar. The quality of the advice and the service you receive from your advisor should be worth the fees you are paying.

## PAST PERFORMANCE IS NOT A PREDICTOR OF FUTURE PERFORMANCE

At the bottom of mutual fund advertisements is a disclaimer that might read something like this: "Past performance does not guarantee future results. Future performance may be higher or lower than in the past." This is a very truthful and factual statement. Although past performance can provide some information about a fund, it gives no information about how it will do in the future. You should never buy a fund strictly based on its past performance. There are ample studies that show that a fund that is a top performer one year can just as easily be a poor performer the next.

Mutual fund ranking services, such as Morningstar, rate funds using a five-star scale. These rankings are based on past performance and volatility and should not be considered as a promise of future performance.

## What you can do now

- Review all your mutual fund holdings.
- Calculate the fees you pay for mutual funds.
- Determine if each mutual fund is still appropriate for your portfolio and ask yourself why you should still own it.
- Examine the past performance of each fund.

- If a mutual fund is less than 5 percent of your overall portfolio, it is probably an insignificant holding. Consider either redeeming it or adding to the position.

## The bottom line

Mutual funds are the investment of choice for many Canadians and, like any investment, they have advantages and disadvantages. It is important to make an informed decision when buying a mutual fund to ensure that it is appropriate for you. You want to be satisfied that it will complement other investments in your portfolio and that it can reasonably be expected to perform better than the average fund in its class.

# Rule 30

## Consider the Advantages and Disadvantages of Individual Stocks and Bonds

Prior to the 1980s, when mutual funds were almost unknown, most investors bought and held individual securities such as common stocks, preferred shares, or bonds. You can still build your portfolio this way. One
advantage of this investment strategy is that it is simple to understand and
the fees and commissions are transparent. For those who like to buy and
hold individual securities, the cost of maintaining a portfolio can be quite
low. This is especially true for those who manage their portfolio themselves.
Many people view managing their own investments as a hobby. They enjoy
the research, the analysis of stocks and the market, and the "action." Retirees
who enjoy the market have the time necessary to devote to it. There is no
reason why people with the proper skill, knowledge, and interest should not
do well with a portfolio of individual securities. However, investors who do
this face three challenges: becoming overloaded with information, ensuring proper diversification, and believing that beating the market is easy.

### INFORMATION OVERLOAD

Today, the average investor is drowning in information. With all the statistics, reports, and commentary available, it becomes exceedingly difficult to
sort out the "noise" from the material that is truly valuable. More than ever,
investors need to follow a disciplined investment strategy and focus on
the important information that will allow them to make sound investment
decisions with confidence. Fear, greed, regret, and inertia can negatively
influence financial decisions, but a sound and rational investment strategy
can lessen their impact.

### PROPER DIVERSIFICATION

A properly diversified portfolio is one of the keys to long-term financial
success. All investors can control how well their portfolio is diversified,
but most of them fail at the task. While investors who own mutual funds
tend to be overdiversified, those who buy individual securities tend to be
underdiversified. It is not unusual for them to have high concentration

in one sector, such as bank stocks, energy stocks, or income trusts. Many investors might have a portfolio of Canadian stocks with no bonds or international securities.

There are a number of reasons why portfolios are not properly diversified. One reason is simply that investors do not understand how to construct one; it does require some skill and understanding of the market and investing. The other reason is that many people are momentum investors—they focus on those stocks that have been doing well recently, with the net result of overexposure to one stock, one sector, or one type of investment. For example, many investors had large positions in technology stocks just before the bubble burst in 2000–2001. More recently, many investors, particularly retirees, were over-concentrated in income trusts.

Some people have a familiarity bias. They will invest in what they know and understand. An individual who is very knowledgeable about the biotechnology industry might have more investments in that sector than would be prudent, even for the most aggressive investor. Similarly, a Canadian might have a "home" bias, with a portfolio containing all Canadian stock, even though Canada represents only about 3 percent of all companies worldwide.

One problem for those who invest strictly in individual stocks and bonds is obtaining the international exposure necessary for a properly diversified portfolio. Even if you could do the research to track down the best stocks in Europe, Latin America, and the Far East, trading them on the different stock exchanges with different currencies would be very difficult, if not impossible.

## TRYING TO BEAT THE MARKET

In theory, it seems like it should be an easy task to pick a few stocks that will do better than the market. In practice, this is very difficult to do, much like it is difficult to go to Las Vegas frequently and always come back with more money in your wallet than when you left home. We are not saying that it is impossible for the average individual to beat the market, particularly for short periods of time; rather, we are saying that it is very difficult for the average investor to beat the market consistently over extended periods of time.

The average investor has about the same chance, over the longer term, of consistently beating the professional investors as a good golfer has of consistently beating a PGA-tour pro. In the investing world, the professionals are the investment counsellors and mutual fund managers, the huge pension plans, and the trading desks of the large market players who trade for their own accounts. The large traders include banks such as the Royal Bank and Citibank, and brokerage firms such as BMO Nesbitt Burns and Goldman Sachs. These firms employ thousands of Ph.D.s and professional traders, and they have invested hundreds of millions of dollars in their trading systems. They have more experience, more tools, and more information than individual investors. Still, on any given day, half of these professionals will be wrong. Those who are exceptional, the real winners of this group, are those who might, over the long term, be wrong only 45 percent of the time!

## What you can do now

- Identify the investing style and strategy you use when buying and selling stocks. If you cannot state your strategy, then you do not have one.
- Review your current holdings to determine if you should buy, hold, or sell.
- Do a sector analysis of the stock holding, looking for sectors that are either over-concentrated or under-represented.
- Begin researching, reading, and analyzing the market. You will need to do this on a regular basis.
- Ask yourself what skill you have that will enable you to beat the pros at their own game.

## The bottom line

Building an investment portfolio bottom up with the use of individual stocks and bonds is a reasonable approach for many investors, especially those who like the "action" and the research involved. However, there are challenges. You need a sound investment strategy to ensure a properly diversified portfolio that allows you to sort out the "noise" from the "information" and to lessen the risk of your emotions getting the better of you.

# Rule 31

## Learn about Exchange Traded Funds (The Simple Solution)

Compared to other investment products, exchange traded funds are a relatively new phenomenon; unlike most trends, this one did not start south of the border, but in Canada. The Toronto Stock Exchange created the first exchange traded funds, called the TIPS and HIPS, in 1992. Investors could buy a fund consisting of the shares of companies that made up the TSE 35 and TSE 100 Composite Indexes. Since then, the growth has been strong around the world. By the end of December 2007, there were 1,171 ETFs worldwide, trading on 39 different stock exchanges, with assets of almost $800 billion.

Typically, ETFs try to replicate a stock market index such as the S&P 500 or the S&P/TSX 60 Composite Index. This method of investing is called indexing or passive management. In Canada, institutional investors use this strategy more frequently than individual investors. In the Benefits Canada 2007 survey of the top 100 pension plans in Canada, the 100 largest plans had $316.6 billion invested in Canadian equities, U.S. equities, and Canadian bonds. Of that amount, $88.3 billion, or 27.9 percent of the total, was indexed.

The amount indexed by retail investors is likely to be below 1 percent. There are several explanations for this difference. For one thing, most average investors are not aware of the benefits of indexing and don't know how to do it. For another, investments are typically "sold" rather than "bought," and there is no incentive for an advisor to "sell" low-cost investments for the small investor. And, finally, many retail investors and their advisors are confident in their active management investment skills and knowledge and believe that they can "beat" the market. Whatever the reason, it is hard to imagine that the experienced professionals who run the multi-billion dollar pension funds and index part of their assets are wrong and all the individual investors who don't are right. Indexing part, if not all, of the investment portfolio is something that the average investor should consider, and using exchange traded funds is a simple, cost-effective way of doing it.

ETFs represent shares of ownership in either funds or unit investment trusts that hold portfolios of common stocks or bonds. They are designed to generally correspond to the price and yield performance of their under-lying indexes. ETFs give investors the opportunity to buy or sell an entire portfolio of stocks or bonds in a single security, as easily as buying or sell-ing a share of stock.

ETFs have significantly lower annual expense ratios than most other investment products. They are less likely to have high management fees because they are index-based rather than actively managed. In Canada, the annual management fees are typically between 0.20 percent and 0.75 per-cent. The lowest-cost ETF, the iShares S&P/TSX 60 Composite Index, has a MER of 0.17 percent. On a $100,000 investment, this would mean a fee of $170 per year, versus $2,500 per year in a typical mutual fund.

Since ETFs are generally designed to correspond to the performance of their underlying index or commodity, you will always know exactly what you're buying—the index that the ETF is designed to replicate. A mutual fund, on the other hand, has to report its holdings only twice a year. There could be a major difference between what you thought you were buying and what you actually bought.

ETFs are priced and traded throughout the day at any time the stock exchange is open, in contrast to mutual funds, whose price is set at the end of the day. If you placed your order to buy a mutual fund at the beginning of the day and the price rose throughout the day, you would be forced to pay the higher price.

Because each ETF is comprised of a basket of securities, it automatically provides diversification across an entire index. Additionally, the expand-ing universe of ETFs in Canada and the U.S. covers a diverse variety of markets, including:

- broad-based equity indexes such as large-cap growth and small-cap value
- broad-based international and country-specific equity indexes such as Europe and EAFE (Europe, Australia, and the Far East)
- industry-sector-specific equity indexes such as gold, financial, and materials
- bond indexes such as long-term government bonds and corporate bonds
- commodities such as gold, silver, and oil

ETFs, like index funds in general, tend to offer greater tax benefits because they generate fewer capital gains due to the low turnover of the securities that comprise the portfolio. In general, an ETF sells securities only to reflect changes in its underlying index. Thus, ETFs tend to be more tax efficient than actively managed mutual funds.

## U.S. ETFS

Since exchange traded funds trade like stocks, it is just as easy to buy a U.S. ETF as it is to buy one that trades in Canada. The U.S. has a great variety of ETFs. By the first quarter of 2007, 469 ETFs were listed in the U.S. and over 330 were about to be listed.

Canadians cannot buy mutual funds that are sold in the U.S. They can buy only from mutual fund companies registered in Canada. For example, Fidelity has a mutual fund in the U.S. called the Disciplined Equity Fund. The company distributes a similar fund in Canada called the American Disciplined Equity Fund. In the U.S., the MER of this fund is only 0.91 percent, but in Canada investors can buy only the one that is registered here and has an MER of 2.35 percent. On the other hand, Canadian investors can buy U.S. ETFs, paying the same low fees as American investors.

## DISADVANTAGES OF ETFS COMPARED TO MUTUAL FUNDS

One advantage that managed mutual funds have over ETFs is that a mutual fund manager can take a defensive position and move from stocks to cash if she believes that a stock market meltdown is imminent. In theory at least, if the manager is alert, the drop in value of a mutual fund portfolio might be less than the drop in an ETF portfolio at the time of a stock market crash. An ETF will never outperform its benchmark but at any given time there will be a number of mutual funds that will.

### What you can do now

- Investigate the various ETFs available in the U.S. and Canada.
- If you don't have ETFs in your portfolio, ask your advisor why.
- Analyze your current portfolio to determine how ETFs might be incorporated into it.

## The bottom line

Passive management or indexing is an investment management approach that allows investors to duplicate the performance of an underlying index like the S&P 500. With exchange traded funds, individual investors are able to match the performance of the overall market, something institutional investors have been doing for many years.

# Rule 32

## Use a Core/Satellite Investment Strategy

If you are investing with individual securities, how can you properly diversify your portfolio when you are purchasing only a small number of stocks? The answer is to use an investment approach called core/satellite, which allows you to combine both an index and individual stocks. To provide diversification, you use ETFs, which form the "core" of the portfolio. Then you select individual stocks that are expected to outperform the benchmark to form the "satellites" around the ETFs. Typically, an investor might put 50 percent of his equity portfolio in an ETF representing a market index and 50 percent in individual securities. There is no hard and fast rule about the percentages. However, the greater the percentage of the portfolio in the core holding, the more the overall portfolio will behave like the overall market.

Although they might not admit it, most portfolio managers take a core/satellite approach when managing their Canadian equity portfolio. Since these managers are judged against the performance of the overall market, they are always acutely aware of how much their portfolio resembles or deviates from it. They are diversified across all industrial sectors. The part of their portfolio that mirrors the overall market can be considered the "core" and the part that deviates from the overall market can be considered the "satellite." When you hear portfolio managers say that they are trading around their "core" bank holdings, or that they are currently overweight oil stocks and underweight technology stocks, or that they have a small-cap tilt to their portfolio, they are essentially taking the core/satellite approach.

### REASONS TO CONSIDER A CORE/SATELLITE INVESTMENT STRATEGY

We believe the majority of individual investors who currently hold individual stocks in their portfolio would benefit from this strategy for the following reasons.

**THERE IS BETTER DIVERSIFICATION OF RISK:** Typically, the average investor who buys stock tends to have a poorly diversified portfolio. They often have a concentration in sectors or types of stocks with very similar risk characteristics. Using an ETF to buy a core position will provide instant diversification and reduce the overall risk of the portfolio.

**IT IS EASIER TO MONITOR AND UNDERSTAND THE RISK:** The more stocks a portfolio contains, the harder it is to monitor and understand the risk. More investment decisions have to be made and more factors have to be considered. With an ETF or index fund representing a core position, the number of stocks can be decreased, resulting in a simpler portfolio.

**IT IS MORE TAX EFFICIENT:** A portfolio that contains all stocks will tend to generate more trading activity as the market and investment outlook change. With more trading activity, more capital gains will be realized and more taxes paid. With a larger proportion of the portfolio in a single core holding, fewer capital gains will be triggered.

**THE TRANSACTION COSTS ARE LOWER:** With fewer stocks, there will be fewer trades and fewer commissions. The small annual management fee of the ETF will easily be recovered from the savings on commissions. In an account at a full-service broker, the reduction of commissions could be dramatic. (This could be why most investment advisors do not like ETFs.)

**THE VOLATILITY IS DECREASED:** For the typical investor with an ETF representing a core holding, the overall portfolio will likely be less volatile than one made up entirely of stocks.

**IT ALLOWS THE INVESTOR TO FOCUS HIS ATTENTION ON MONEY-MAKING IDEAS:** In any well-designed portfolio, a person will have to invest in sectors or stocks that he does not like, but that he needs for diversification purposes. Using an ETF for a core position provides the necessary diversification, allowing the investor to focus on those stocks that he likes in those sectors where he expects to be able to outperform.

**IT IMPROVES THE PERFORMANCE OF THE PORTFOLIO:** After costs, over 50 percent of professional money managers will, on average, underperform the market. The average individual investor typically fares worse. Therefore, by reducing your stock portfolio and replacing part of it with a core holding, you will more likely than not improve the overall performance of your portfolio while reducing its risk.

**ASSET MIX CHANGES BECOME EASIER:** A change in an investor's asset mix is easier to implement when he uses an ETF as the core position. If an investor wants to increase his equity exposure, the purchase of additional shares of an ETF makes it easy to do without having to research individual stocks.

**THE INVESTOR CAN IMPLEMENT SOPHISTICATED STRATEGIES:** Investment strategies such as enhanced index strategies, risk budgeting, portfolio insurance, style tilts, hedging strategies, and tax loss harvesting become easier to implement with a core/satellite approach.

**IT MAKES YOU A BETTER INVESTOR:** The proper implementation of a core/satellite strategy requires a certain degree of knowledge and understanding about risk, market indexes, benchmarks, and portfolio management techniques. As people gain the knowledge and experience needed to apply a core/satellite strategy, the process makes them better investors.

## What you can do now

- Analyze your current portfolio and identify which part is the core and which part would be considered the satellite position.
- Determine where your strengths lie in managing your portfolio.
- Review available ETFs and consider how to incorporate them into your portfolio.

## The bottom line

With the advent of inexpensive ETFs, people who typically buy individual stocks and bonds can improve the overall quality of their investment portfolio with a core/satellite strategy, using a broad-based ETF as the core and selecting individual stocks or more specialized mutual funds or ETFs as the satellite position. This will allow investors to receive broad-based diversification and add money-making ideas as well.

# Rule 33

## Understand the Investments Specifically Targeted at Retirees

Leading up to retirement, people become more focused on investment products and strategies to help accumulate wealth. However, once retired, people's investment needs and risk profiles change, and the focus switches to strategies to convert the wealth into income for retirement. The growth in the number of baby boomers approaching retirement has not gone unnoticed by the "new-products" division of the financial services industry. As a result, we are finding many new and some not-so-new investment products specifically designed for retirees. The number of new products designed for "distributing" income in retirement is expected to increase dramatically in the future. It is important to understand how these products work to determine if they will meet your new needs.

### CONSIDER A LIFE ANNUITY

An annuity is one of many income options available for retirees. Most individuals will, in fact, collect an annuity whether they bought one or not. The Old Age Security, CPP, and company pension plans that pay a monthly income are a type of life annuity. It is essentially a contract between the customer and the issuer (an insurance company), providing the customer a set amount of income based on his desired payment schedule. A life annuity provides the customer or annuitant a guaranteed monthly or annual payment until she dies. The payments will cease on death regardless of the length of time the annuity was in place.

There are two features that make annuities very attractive for retirees. The first is that they provide a protection against longevity risk. Someone who purchases a life annuity is guaranteed income from his annuity as long as he lives. The second feature is that a life annuity will provide a higher amount of guaranteed monthly income than any other investment choice at any given point in time. This is because part of the monthly income is a return of the capital that is invested in the annuity. And if you live longer than average, you will, in effect, also receive a return of capital of those who died at a younger age than average. The downside is that on death, the payments cease and the estate is left with nothing. (This is no different from how your OAS or CPP payments work.)

There are many different types of annuities, each with different benefits, guarantees, and risks. The most common ones—a straight life annuity and a joint and last survivor annuity—are discussed below.

### FACTORS THAT AFFECT A LIFE ANNUITANT'S PAYOUT

The amount of annual income an annuitant receives will depend on a number of factors, including the person's age and sex, current interest rates, and mortality tables.

The younger the annuitant, the longer he is expected to live and the lower the payments. There is no reason for those who have just retired to buy an annuity right away. They can get one when they're older— assuming interest rates do not drop, the payment will be higher.

The implied interest rate applied or assumed in calculating the annuity is based on the general level of interest rates in place when the annuity is purchased. The higher the interest rates, the higher the monthly payments. It is always best to buy annuities when interest rates are high so that you can lock in the higher rate for life.

Insurance companies base their annuity payments on an actuarial assessment of their clients. The average life expectancy of the annuitant is a key variable in determining the monthly payout.

Women on average are expected to outlive men, so annuity payments to women are lower than those to men of the same age. A joint and last survivor annuity will pay a lower amount than a single life annuity.

### THE DECISION TO BUY AN ANNUITY

When retirees are contemplating purchasing a life annuity, they face a dilemma. They have spent many years building up an investment port-folio for retirement. It is difficult to relinquish control of their nest egg, particularly if they see themselves as wise investors. However, people also like the benefit of guaranteed income and generally feel happier and more secure for it. For many people, it is the financial peace of mind they know they will get from purchasing an annuity that wins them over.

One way to think about the purchase of an annuity is in terms of diversification. A well-diversified portfolio will have both fixed-income investments and equity investments. Within the category of fixed-income investments there should also be diversification. This might mean having corporate bonds as well as government bonds, and short-term as well as long-term maturities. For practical purposes, a life annuity is very similar to a very long-term government bond. One difference is that you can always decide to sell the bond and take the cash for personal use or to buy another investment. But when you buy a life annuity, you give your capital to the insurance company in exchange for payments that are guaranteed for as long you live. A life annuity can be considered as part of an overall portfolio, suggesting that it might make good sense to invest 5 to 20 percent of your financial assets in one. There is no need to buy an annuity in one lump payment. You can create additional diversification by buying several smaller annuities at different times.

Another way of using an annuity is to help provide the monthly income required to maintain your basic needs. You would buy an annuity in an amount that would cover your basic living expenses when added to your CPP and OAS. You would then invest the rest of your capital in a regular portfolio that will allow you to take money out for any purpose at any time. Since the annuity provides a guarantee of some income, you may invest more aggressively with the remainder of the portfolio to provide protection against inflation.

The main consideration in determining whether or not to buy an annuity is your general health and life expectancy. The better your health, and the longer you expect to live, the better value an annuity becomes. Your longevity is an important factor, if not the most important one, in deciding to buy an annuity. Individuals who choose to annuitize part of their income tend to be healthier and live longer than those who do not. It is not that buying annuities is good for your health, but that those in poor health with short life expectancies do not buy annuities. Of course the insurance companies know this, so they assume that annuity buyers will live longer than average and take that into consideration when they set their prices. Each insurance company will have different mortality experience and will make a different set of assumptions when pricing the annuity. Therefore, those contemplating purchasing annuities should shop around and get the best price possible.

## REVERSE MORTGAGES

Many Canadians have substantial equity in their homes at the time of retirement. Most retirees want to stay in their own home, but some will have inadequate income or financial resources to deal with essential day-to-day needs or emergencies. This is the common situation known as being "house rich and cash poor." The advantage of a reverse mortgage is that it enables you to stay in your home and maintain your desired lifestyle even though you have insufficient income from other sources. You are effectively tapping into some of the equity in the home without having to sell it.

A reverse mortgage is a loan against your home that you do not have to pay back until you sell the house or die. To be eligible, homeowners must be 62 or older. Unlike a conventional mortgage, there is no minimum income requirement. The amount of the loan is generally 25 to 30 percent of the value of the dwelling and is based on the age of the borrower, the current level of interest rates, the value of the home, and the anticipated interest rates. The interest and principal of the loan will compound, so the amount owing on the mortgage can add up quickly. People with reverse mortgages will be faced with rising debt and falling equity in the future. If you are looking at the house as the "ace in the hole" and planning to use the equity to fund your retirement living, you have to be careful; a reverse mortgage may mean the equity in the home will be used up by the time the house is sold. It is possible for the loan and the accumulated interest to exceed the value of the property. However, the homeowners, or their estates, will not be asked to pay more than the value of the home, and they will never be forced to leave.

Taking out a reverse mortgage involves many associated costs. To begin with, the interest paid on the loan is typically 1.5 percent above the regular interest rates of a conventional five-year mortgage; the rate is changed annually and interest is compounded semi-annually. There are legal, appraisal, and administration fees as well. They are generally above $1,200.

A reverse mortgage is an expensive way to borrow money and generally should be considered only as a last resort after all other liquid assets have been depleted. At the moment, it is not common practice among Canadian retirees. The Canadian Home Income Plan, a leading national provider of reverse mortgages, has placed only about 11,000 reverse mortgages since 1986; this represents a small fraction of the millions of senior homeowners.

From a straight financial perspective for those who require equity from their home, downsizing and moving to a smaller house usually makes more economic sense than taking out a mortgage. However, many people have a strong emotional attachment to their home and neighbourhood. Wanting to stay there is not so much a financial decision as an emotional one. If you do decide to take out a reverse mortgage, it is prudent to get some financial counselling beforehand so you will understand both the benefits and the drawbacks.

### LIFE CYCLE/TARGET DATE FUNDS

A life cycle fund is a relatively new type of "balanced" mutual fund. The asset mix of the fund is systematically adjusted to become more and more conservative as the investor approaches the planned retirement date. Life cycle funds are generally made up of other mutual funds rather than individual stocks or bonds.

Life cycle funds are also called target date funds because each fund has a target retirement date that matches the individual's planned date of retirement. If you were going to retire in 2010, you would pick Target 2010. With these funds the investor does nothing; the asset mix adjustments are made automatically. In theory, this allows you to always be wisely invested, free from the need to make decisions or let emotions get in the way of sensible choices. This simplicity is a big attraction at a time when other investment products are becoming more complicated. Compared to what many investors are using now, the life cycle fund is an improvement. The downside is that people have different tolerances for risk and different requirements in terms of what rate of return they need to earn to achieve their goals. These tolerances and requirements are independent of a person's age.

The life cycle funds focus on the period up to retirement. There appear to be fewer offerings for people who are already retired or who will retire within a few years. The funds assume that the asset mix that is appropriate at the date of retirement will also be appropriate for the next 25 to 35 years. In our view, most of the target funds have a higher level of equities than is wise or necessary in the early years leading up to retirement and not enough equities to provide inflation protection in the retirement years. Life cycle funds have not been around long enough to draw a definitive conclusion about their appropriateness for retirees.

If you are considering a life cycle fund, it is critical that you understand what the present asset allocation is and how it will change over the next 5, 10, 20, and 30 years. There is a significant difference in asset allocation (offered by Morningstar) between some of the major life cycle fund providers; for example, Fidelity ClearPath 2010 and Clarington Target Click 2010. In March 2007, Fidelity ClearPath 2010 had an allocation of 41 percent equities and 59 percent cash and fixed income, while Clarington Target Click 2010 had an allocation of 6 percent equities and 94 percent cash and fixed income. Each life cycle fund also has a different "glidepath," which determines the rate the fund moves from equities to bonds. Each company has its own philosophy and mathematical equations for arriving at the glidepath.

Some investors own many other types of mutual funds on top of a target date fund; they lose some of the benefits of the target date funds if they are diversifying in other funds. As with other investments, people should consider all the pertinent information about life cycle funds before deciding whether they it are appropriate for them.

### STRUCTURED NOTES WITH GUARANTEES

There are many different types of structured products. Most of them guarantee a return of your capital after 6 to 10 years. In addition to this, you can expect to receive an annual income and a capital gain at maturity because your investment is linked to another asset class, such as common stocks, indexes, mutual funds, baskets of mutual funds, and even hedge funds. One problem with structured products is the level of complexity inherent in their design. Because all of these investments are different, it takes a lot of work and time to understand the pros and cons of any particular one.

One of the most common structured products is called a principal-protected note (PPN). Typically, PPNs guarantee 100 percent of invested capital as long as the note is held to maturity. This means that no matter what happens to the markets, you will receive all your money back at maturity, plus any appreciation from the underlying assets. At maturity, if the linked asset has gone up in value by 20 percent, you will (in theory) also get a gain of 20 percent.

The guarantee is the economic equivalent of a zero coupon bond. Sixty-five to 70 percent of the invested amount is used to fund the guarantee. The other 30 to 35 percent is invested in the underlying linked assets. Usually some form of option strategy is used to gain the leverage. In essence, a PPN is a synthetic investment made up of derivative products. These financially engineered products are very difficult for the average investor or advisor to understand fully.

The Canadian Securities Administrators, made up of representatives of the Securities Regulators across Canada, have become worried about the proliferation of PPNs in recent years. They expressed their concerns in CSA Notice 46–303, which was widely distributed. They noted that, "Recent types of PPN products are more complex and pose investment risks that investors may not be fully informed about." The notice went on to say that sales and marketing material did not contain "sufficient information to allow an investor to understand how much the underlying investments would need to return, after fees, to deliver the upside that was promoted . . . information statements provided for many PPNs were lengthy, complex and difficult to understand . . . describing the methods used to deliver principal protection and the upside benefit of the return on the linked investment."

Like other very complex investment products, principal-protected notes are very profitable for the companies who manufacture and distribute them. PPNs are not regulated in the same fashion as mutual funds; consequently the seller can withhold information about fees. These fees include commissions of about 5 percent, structuring fees, annual management fees, guarantee fees, early redemption fees, trailer fees, and performance fees. These costs will definitely dampen overall performance. For example, a PPN typically has a commission of 5 percent built in to the selling price, so if you buy a note for $100, only $95 is invested; essentially, the note will have to go up by 5.25 percent for you to break even. Most, if not all, of the PPN's fees are embedded in the pricing structure, hidden from unsuspecting buyers. This fact, added to the complexity of the product, allows for its sponsors to charge high total fees.

PPNs are examples of complex, financially engineered investment products sold to unsophisticated investors. If you have a well-diversified, effectively managed portfolio, you have nothing to gain by purchasing PPNs, especially if you do not fully understand them. A simple rule of thumb is that if you do not understand all the details of an investment product, you cannot afford to buy it.

## What you can do now

- Be leery of all products with guarantees and understand fully what you are getting into before you buy them.
- Understand all products that are used to "distribute" income and capital in retirement.
- If you do not understand some of the newer products, seek some unbiased financial advice.

## The bottom line

Today, there are a number of products designed specifically to save money for retirement or to distribute income after retirement. We expect the number of these products to increase dramatically over the next few years. Many of these new products are complex and financially engineered and are geared to unsophisticated investors. It is very important to understand fully what you are buying.

# Part 7

## Monitor and Manage
## Your Investments Wisely

EVERYONE HAS A DIFFERENT LEVEL OF INTEREST AND EXPERIENCE IN INVESTMENTS and their management. Some people are passionate about the subject. They enjoy doing the research and following the daily fluctuations in the stock market and the economy. They read their monthly statements closely. They are experienced, knowledgeable, have an excellent understanding of the issues, and are fully engaged in managing their investments. Other people have no interest whatsoever in the investment process and are unaware of what is happening in the markets or the economy. They find it a chore even to open their monthly statements. They have limited knowledge about investments, and little or no understanding of the issues and the risks involved in their management.

Although investors have different levels of interest and knowledge, they do share common objectives. They all want to see their investments managed effectively and they want to achieve their financial goals. These objectives are critical for retirees, who rely on their investments for much of their income. Keep in mind that knowledge and experience do not guarantee investment success. It is certainly possible for people with limited interest and experience in investing to do just as well, if not better, than experienced investors who are involved in the process on a day-to-day basis.

# Rule 34

## Determine the Role You Want to Take in Managing Your Investments

To get the best results from your investments, you need to understand your strengths and weaknesses and to define the role you will take in the investment process. The role you choose depends on your level of interest, involvement, skill, and experience.

With the advent of online trading, instant portfolio valuations, multiple investment options, and online help from experts, managing your investments has never been easier, and it is a sensible choice for many people. These do-it-yourselfers may decide to take on all of the roles available, including investment analyst, portfolio manager, and securities trader. Another option is to work with a financial advisor who, in most cases, is a commissioned salesperson. The third option is to delegate all of the investment decision making to a discretionary portfolio manager or investment counsellor. For a fee, this person will take full responsibility for professionally managing your investments.

Investors can be divided into four groups based on their knowledge and level of involvement.

### KNOWLEDGEABLE AND INVOLVED INVESTORS

These are people who have the time, the knowledge, and the inclination to look after their investments themselves. They may be working with an advisor, but could easily do the job themselves. Those who work with an advisor often enjoy the relationship and like to have someone to discuss the markets with. They are on an even footing with the advisor, so they understand, and can properly evaluate, any investment recommendations they receive. They could move their money to an investment counsellor, who would manage it professionally on a discretionary basis, but they might miss the action. These types of investors are free to choose how they manage their money. Those who decide to manage it themselves or to work with an advisor should realize that in retirement their first objective is to meet their financial goals, not to enjoy their hobby.

## KNOWLEDGEABLE AND UNINVOLVED INVESTORS

These investors are knowledgeable about the market but choose not to take an active interest in it. Maybe they travel frequently, or are busy with work or family, or have just lost interest in the area of investing. For some retirees, illness may mean that they are not able to properly attend to their financial affairs. Those investors who want to go it alone or work with an advisor should simplify their investment portfolio with a few well-chosen ETFs or mutual funds. With a simpler portfolio there is less need for an advisor, but it may still make sense to continue the relationship. Other knowledgeable investors may decide it makes sense simply to move their funds to an investment counsellor and delegate all of the responsibility to a qualified professional.

## INVOLVED INVESTORS WITH LIMITED KNOWLEDGE

Typically, this type of investor is new to the field, wants to learn, and wants to get involved. Everyone has to start somewhere, but it would be foolish for these novice investors to go the do-it-yourself route. However, having a professional, such as an investment counsellor, manage your money does not give you a chance to learn or be involved. So working with an advisor is a good place to start. Because your lack of knowledge puts you at a disadvantage in the client/advisor relationship, you need an advisor you can trust. Keeping the investing simple will help you understand what you are doing. The advisor should explain things and educate you to some degree.

## UNINVOLVED INVESTORS WITH LITTLE OR NO KNOWLEDGE

These investors, especially if they are seniors, make vulnerable targets for unscrupulous people. This is particularly true for recently widowed seniors, who are not only coping with grief, but also managing all of the finances. If they do not have the investment knowledge or interest, they are forced to trust those who advise them. These investors are sitting ducks for an unethical advisor, and are at a disadvantage even when dealing with an inexperienced but well-intentioned one. For this type of investor, it is vital to have an experienced advisor whom they trust completely. In many cases, if investors have sufficient funds, they should simply hire a discretionary money manager or investment counsellor to look after their portfolio.

## What you can do now

- Recognize that as a client, setting realistic goals and meeting them is the most important role you can take.
- Do an honest evaluation of your skills and knowledge as an investor.
- Determine how involved you want to be in managing your investments.
- Evaluate your current role and determine if a different approach might be more suitable.
- Be sure you understand the difference between a financial advisor/ salesperson and a professional money manager, such as an investment counsellor.

## The bottom line

It is important for investors to recognize their own strengths and weaknesses. This will help them decide whether to manage their investments themselves, work with an advisor, or delegate the investment decisions to a discretionary portfolio manager or investment counsellor. It is possible for all investors, even those with limited knowledge and interest, to be successful if they delegate their investment decisions properly.

# Rule 35

## Get the Most Out of Working with a Financial Advisor

Financial advisors go by many different names and titles in Canada. They may be called financial planners, investment advisors, or investment consultants. They work for banks, investment dealers, insurance companies, or small independent companies. They sell a variety of insurance products, mutual funds, managed products, stocks, and bonds. The specific products they offer will depend upon the type of firm they work for and what they are registered to sell. Some advisors might be licensed to sell only one type of product, while others can sell them all. We estimate that there are approximately 85,000 financial advisors in Canada. For many investors, the financial advisor acts as their interface with the investment world.

There are two important things to know about this group. First, the legal registration of nearly every advisor in Canada is actually that of "salesperson." Most advisors are compensated by transaction commissions and/or management fees from mutual funds or wrap accounts. All of the advice they give is, essentially, free; they get paid when you act on their advice. Second, advisors can buy and sell securities only when directed by the client. Advisors cannot protect clients from themselves. If a client wants to do something that is foolish or risky and the advisor cannot talk him out of doing it, the responsibility of the action lies with the client.

Providing investment advice and buying and selling securities is a profitable business. Usually, the advisor will proactively make recommendations or provide advice. Rarely does a client phone up her advisor with a shopping list of investments. The more advice the advisor gives that results in a transaction, the more money he makes. Once the client approves the trade, the result of the transaction inevitably becomes her responsibility. As long as the advisor did not misrepresent the investment advice or do anything illegal, there is no recourse for the client. We believe that most financial advisors are interested in doing the right thing for their clients. We also believe that advisors who are experienced, prudent, and have the client's best interests at heart can help most individuals manage their investments. However, lack of accountability and a compensation system based on quantity of revenue rather than quality of advice can lead to a conflict of interest.

## TYPES OF ADVISORS

Every advisor is different and each brings to the table different levels of knowledge and experience. Advisors all have different approaches to investing.

Client-centric advisors see their role as helping the client to clarify his goals and creating an investment portfolio that can be expected to achieve those goals with the least possible risk. These advisors put their client's interests first, charge reasonable fees, and try to deliver true value for their services.

Advisor-centric advisors get into the business to make money and are primarily focused on maximizing their commissions or fees. They see their clients as profit centres and, like all good businesspeople, their goal is to maximize their revenue. Although they all like to see their clients do well, their own interests come first.

The majority of advisors fit somewhere between these two extremes. They strike a balance between being 100 percent client centric and 100 percent advisor centric. Unfortunately, especially at the beginning of the relationship, an investor can never know for sure where on the continuum the advisor lies.

## HAVE REALISTIC EXPECTATIONS OF WHAT AN ADVISOR CAN DO FOR YOU

No matter which type of advisor you choose, you should be realistic about what this person can do for you. You should expect your advisor to give you a clear explanation of his philosophy and process. Your advisor should provide an overview of the financial markets and potential investment risks, as well as be willing to provide continual education and to act as a sounding board for your ideas. Your advisor should also tell you how your portfolio is performing compared to an agreed-upon benchmark.

Since it is difficult for even the best portfolio managers to outperform the markets on a consistent basis, you should not expect your advisor to do so. Most advisors will not have the education, experience, or knowledge that a portfolio manager has. In addition, the high fees and transaction costs inherent in typical retail investment products are another barrier that makes it difficult for even the most experienced and competent advisor to consistently outperform. However, your advisor should, as a minimum, provide you with good service and advice that is appropriate for your investment objectives and risk tolerance.

To make the relationship work, you should provide full disclosure of your financial assets and your financial goals and objectives. The goals should be both honest and realistic. Communication is critical for a good relationship, and both positive and negative feedback will help to develop a more honest and open relationship.

## BE AWARE OF CONFLICT OF INTEREST

Unfortunately, the reality of the financial services industry is that companies and financial advisors all have the potential for a serious conflict of interest. This potential manifests itself through higher than necessary fees, more active trading in an account, and/or higher risk than necessary in investment portfolios. While most financial advisors put their clients' interests first, there is no way they can totally eliminate the conflict of interest in the system. It is up to investors to be vigilant by actively monitoring their accounts, seeing how performance compares to the benchmark, and questioning fees and frequent trading. Clients should always ensure that investments are appropriate for them and seek lower-cost investment solutions.

We believe that when you are working with an advisor, there are two simple things you can do to help reduce the potential conflict of interest, improve communication, and ensure that your financial goals are met. The first is to develop a written investment plan called an investment policy statement (IPS). The second is to insist that you get a regular report on the performance of the portfolio compared to the benchmark. This will help ensure that your investment goals are met. If they are not, the report will show you what you have to do to get back on track. Also, for those who rely heavily on the opinion of an advisor, the report provides a quantitative measure of the quality of the advice.

## INSIST ON AN INVESTMENT POLICY STATEMENT

An IPS goes a long way towards ensuring a harmonious relationship with your financial advisor. It sets out the details of the way your account will be managed. An IPS includes a statement of goals and objectives, the allocation between different asset classes, any investment restrictions, investment strategies, investment fees, the expected long-term target rate of return, the expected range of returns, the rebalancing strategy, and a schedule for account reviews.

The IPS essentially sets out the rules or policies that will determine how your account will be managed. It clearly states the responsibilities of the person and the firm providing the advice. It is an important part of assuring that a proper investment plan and process is in place. Setting out the rules and responsibilities ahead of time will make it easier for both you and your advisor to manage the account. It isn't surprising that all pension plans, foundations, and endowments use an investment policy statement to provide direction for the management of their investment portfolios.

## MONITOR PORTFOLIO PERFORMANCE

Measuring the performance of your portfolio is an essential part of the ongoing investment process. Knowing the rate of return you've earned is the first piece of performance information you need, but you also need more. In order to judge whether or not your portfolio is being well managed you need to be able to compare it to a reference point. One of the most important things in the IPS is a clear statement of the benchmark against which performance will be measured. When you and your advisor agree, in advance, on the benchmark, it is easy to see if your advisor is adding or subtracting value. If the actual results are above benchmark performance, then he or she has added value.

Most investors do not receive performance information on their investment statement. Without this information it is difficult to manage their investment portfolios effectively and to measure the quality of the advice they are receiving. We can only speculate on why this information is not forthcoming. We believe that the managers running the banks and brokerage firms are very intelligent businesspeople who are always looking at ways to improve profits. If they do not provide this information, there must be a sound business reason for the decision. We find it curious, at best, that the large financial institutions that are making billions of dollars from people's investments do not provide the necessary information to help them effectively manage your investments.

Even if you ask for an investment policy statement and a quarterly performance report, there is no guarantee that your financial advisor will provide them. Some advisors may be unwilling to do so because it requires too much work, or they may simply deem it unimportant. Some might be unable to do it because they do not know how, or their firm does not have the ability to calculate portfolio returns.

## What can you do now

- To ensure that your interests and your advisor's are aligned, request an investment policy statement.
- Ask for a regular report that compares your portfolio's performance to the proper benchmark.
- Ask your advisor to itemize all the fees and commissions he or she has earned from your account.
- Go to www.secondopinion.ca/tools/advisorscoreland.aspx to see how the score you give your advisor compares with that of other investors.

## The bottom line

Most advisors have their clients' best interests at heart. However, because most advisors are paid based on transaction fees and commissions, this can result in a conflict of interest.

# Rule 36

## Don't Be Afraid to Do It Yourself (If You Want To)

If you are debating the pros and cons of managing your own investments, you should be aware that managing your money wisely is less complicated than the financial industry would have you believe. You can be certain that no one will have as much enthusiasm for or interest in the long-term results as you. So what holds investors back from trying to manage their money themselves?

### THINKING IT'S TOO COMPLICATED

One of the unfortunate myths that keeps investors from taking charge of their financial security is the belief that managing finances is complicated. Managing an investment portfolio can be extremely complicated—if you want to use futures, options, derivative products, structured products, multiple mutual funds, and investment accounts spread over several different financial institutions. Complicated portfolios are hard to understand, and they generally reduce, rather than enhance, performance. The alternative is a simple portfolio.

In almost every case, a simple portfolio that is properly constructed and widely diversified, consisting of a few professionally managed funds or exchange traded funds, is the best way to go. Table 7.1 on page 216 shows an example of a simple but well diversified $200,000 portfolio. There might be only five investments, but the portfolio has better diversification than most.

This portfolio would be suitable for a balanced investor whose primary goal is growth and for whom income is secondary. It would be practical for an investor who is willing to take average risks for an average return. It is well diversified internationally, and offers excellent balance among Canadian stocks and bonds. The portfolio contains four ETFs invested in four different asset classes with a small cash balance left over.

Assuming this portfolio is bought at an online brokerage firm for $0.03 per share with a $30 minimum, the cost is only $170 or 0.08 percent. If, instead, the $200,000 had been used to purchase a mutual fund from an advisor at a commission of 2 percent, the cost would have been $4,000. The average annual cost of the portfolio above is $403 or 0.20 percent compared to a typical mutual fund fee of 2.5 percent or $5,000. The cost of this ETF portfolio for the first year, including commission, would be $568 compared to the cost of the mutual fund, which would be $9,000!

## TABLE 7.1
### INVESTMENT PORTFOLIO USING ETFS AS OF FEBRUARY 22, 2008

| Symbol | Description | # Shrs | $ Value | Wt % |
|--------|-------------|--------|---------|------|
| Cash | | | 20,652 | 10.3 |
| XBB | iShares Cdn Bond Broad Market Index Fund | 2400 | 69,216 | 34.6 |
| XIU | iShares S&P/TSX 60 Index Fund | 750 | 60,153 | 30 |
| IVV | iShares S&P 500 Index Fund | 220 | 29,902* | 14.9 |
| EFA | iShares MSCI EAFE Index Fund | 280 | 20,073* | 10 |
| Total | | | $200,000 | 100 % |

*These are U.S. securities and assume conversion into Canadian dollars at 1.00

## TABLE 7.2
### FIRST-YEAR COST OF ETF PORTFOLIO

| ETF | # Shrs | $ Value | MER (%) | Fee ($) | Commission ($) |
|-----|--------|---------|---------|---------|----------------|
| Cash | | 20,652 | | | |
| XBB | 2400 | 69,216 | 0.30 | 207 | 72.00 |
| XIU | 750 | 60,153 | 0.17 | 102 | 30.00 |
| IVV | 220 | 29,902 | 0.09 | 27 | 30.00* |
| EFA | 280 | 20,073 | 0.35 | 67 | 30.00* |
| Total | | | 0.20 % | $403 | $170.40 |

*These are U.S. securities and assume conversion into Canadian dollars at 1.00

Not only is this portfolio simple, cheap, and theoretically sound, it is also probably better constructed than the portfolios of 95 percent of other retail investors. In the short-term, it may not outperform all the portfolios of those retail investors, but it will certainly outperform 50 to 60 percent of them. If rebalanced regularly, it might consistently outperform 70 to 80 percent of the other portfolios over the long term. A portfolio like this, which is simple to manage and tax efficient, is not difficult or complicated to construct. It is within the grasp of all investors.

## YOU THINK YOU DON'T HAVE THE TIME

Well, that's about to change. When you retire, you will have more free time and you will need mental activities to keep you sharp. However, you will be surprised to discover how little time maintaining your investments actually takes. After an initial output of time to set up your accounts, the maintenance should not take more than three hours per quarter.

## YOU ARE AFRAID TO MAKE A MISTAKE

If you think that investing involves speculating on small capitalization mining stocks, or finding the next hot geographic region and moving all of your capital to that investment, you will make a big mistake. But if you understand that sensible investing involves diversifying your capital among stocks, bonds, and cash, and if you buy low-fee mutual funds or broadly based ETFs for the stock portion of your portfolio, you are not likely to make a serious mistake. You are more likely to go wrong if you are working with an inexperienced advisor who is trying to sell you structured products, or even worse, suggesting that you use leverage to try to go after even higher returns.

## YOU THINK YOU NEED A LOT OF KNOWLEDGE AND EXPERIENCE

Knowledge and experience are certainly important, but you can develop both by reading two or three good books. There are also many good internet sites that can provide guidance for the do-it-yourself investor. Moreover, there is no guarantee that a financial advisor has more knowledge or experience than you do. Depending on your objectives, managing your money can be very easy or almost impossible. If you think that good money management means beating the market, then you will most likely be disappointed, regardless of whether you do it yourself or use a financial advisor. On the other hand, if you want to match the market, it is very easy to manage your money simply by buying an ETF in whatever market you want to invest.

We believe that beating the market is difficult or impossible to do consistently and that most investors should not even try. Instead, they should aim for a sensibly diversified portfolio made up of stocks and bonds, where the bonds earn interest at the prevailing rate and the stocks give you access to economic growth, both in Canada and around the world.

## YOU BELIEVE YOU NEED TO MAKE CONSTANT TACTICAL CHANGES

You may think you need a financial advisor because you believe only this person knows the best time to buy and sell, and you do not want to take on this responsibility. First, understand that if an advisor really knew when to buy or sell, it would be more profitable for them to trade their own account, rather than work with individual investors. In reality, once the strategic asset mix is determined, and if you are using highly diversified securities such as exchange traded funds, you are not trying to beat or time the market. Then there is no need to do a lot of buying and selling. If retirees understood how seldom portfolios need to be adjusted, they would feel more comfortable taking charge themselves. Tactical changes can be made from time to time, and they may add slightly to the overall portfolio performance, but they are not crucial to good portfolio management.

### What you can do now

- If you currently manage your investments, do an honest evaluation of your performance. Should you continue or should you delegate some or all of the responsibility?
- If you are considering managing your investments by yourself, make sure you have a disciplined approach.
- Determine how you will add value to your investments, whether through superior security selection or asset mix strategies.

### The bottom line

Managing an investment portfolio can be as easy or as difficult as you want. However, the degree of complexity and the amount of time spent managing the investments is no guarantee of success. You can effectively manage your own investments, but you should try to keep the process relatively straightforward. Remember that it is the investment process that determines success, not the investment products; a sound strategy will go a long way towards ensuring success. Those do-it-yourselfers who consistently underperform should consider firing themselves from the active role of managers of their assets. They should take a passive approach, using index funds or exchange traded funds, or else hand the portfolio over to a professional.

# Rule 37

## Delegate Your Investment Decisions to a Professional (If You Want To)

Twenty or 30 years ago, delegating the management of your portfolio to a skilled professional was an option available only to the wealthy. Personal service and customized portfolio management were costly services. However, with the growth in baby boomer wealth and the advent of technology, hiring an investment counsellor is no longer only for the rich. Many people with more modest means will have an account large enough to merit an investment counsellor. Often the fees are lower than those of a typical mutual fund, and in some cases much less.

An investment counsellor's only business is the discretionary management of the investment portfolios of pension plans, endowments, foundations, trusts, estates, and private individuals. Discretionary management of a client's portfolio gives the counsellor the authority to make buy-and-sell decisions on the client's behalf. Managers take this responsibility very seriously. Investment counselling firms range in size from large firms with many employees to single practitioners. However, all must be registered with the securities commission and must abide by a strict code of ethics.

The portfolio managers in the investment counsellor firms differ from financial advisors and mutual fund representatives. They are required by the securities commission to have a higher degree of education and experience in order to manage investment accounts on a discretionary basis. The majority of portfolio managers are members of the Chartered Financial Analysts Institute (CFA), a highly respected international organization that sets strict standards of ethical conduct for the industry. The CFA designation is recognized internationally as the highest standard of education in the investment world.

The minimum account size for investment counsellors can be as low as $100,000, but more typically would be $500,000 to $1,000,000. The management fee for an investment counsellor ranges from 1 to 2 percent at the minimum account size. However, most firms have a sliding scale so that the management of additional assets can be done at a lower cost. For example, on the first $1,000,000 the fee might be 1 percent, but on the next $4,000,000 it might be only 0.75 percent. The total annual fee on a $5,000,000 account using this example would be 0.80 percent.

Investment counsellors, like mutual fund managers, always have a well-articulated investment philosophy and an investment strategy that provides the focus and discipline necessary to manage portfolios effectively. They have a sound investment process that begins with understanding the client's goals and objectives, and they implement a strategy to achieve those goals. They will prepare an investment policy statement specifically for each client. This document provides the guidelines for how the investments will be managed. Part of the process includes regular meetings with the investment counsellor to discuss, among other things, the performance of the portfolio. Because they have discretionary authority over investment decisions, investment counsellors have to adhere to a higher standard of professionalism than the typical advisor. If a large pension plan or foundation can trust its money to an investment counsellor, then an individual investor can feel the same trust.

## What you can do now

- Determine how effectively your portfolio is being managed.
- If you have sufficient funds but limited knowledge of and interest in investing, consider giving your account to an investment counsellor.
- If you are going to use an investment counsellor, interview at least three of them so that you have a good fit.

## The bottom line

If you have enough assets, delegating your investment decisions to an investment counsellor is an excellent option. Whether you are a novice or sophisticated investor, the high standards and professionalism of these experts will ensure that your portfolio is managed effectively, often with lower fees than those of a typical mutual fund.

# Rule 38
## Learn the Seven Steps to a Perfect Portfolio

A PERFECT investment portfolio avoids mistakes in the following areas.

**PLANNING:** *You need blueprints to build a house and you need a financial plan and an investment strategy to build financial security.*

**EDUCATION:** Most investors' opinions come primarily from the mutual fund companies that create investment products or the financial advisors who sell them. *When you receive unbiased advice or an independent second opinion, you often get a totally different perspective on investing.*

**RISK:** *Most investors take more risk than they realize and also more than is necessary.* A common mistake is to compare rates of return without taking into consideration the higher level of risk that was required to earn that higher rate of return.

**FEES:** For someone starting retirement at age 60 with an investment portfolio of $250,000 and who withdraws income and capital until age 90, a reduction of one half of 1 percent could mean $100 more each month for life. *Most investors can save on fees. The first step is to know what you are paying now.*

**EFFICIENT FRONTIER:** Investors should have a portfolio that is *efficient* from a risk and return point of view. Diversification is the key to reducing risk, but you want real diversification—not diworsification. *A common problem is a portfolio that has too many positions and is too complicated to monitor or manage.* The key is to have your investments on the Efficient Frontier— this means having investments that balance one another so that losses in one asset class will be offset by gains in another.

**COMPARISONS:** You can't monitor your portfolio properly or make adjustments to it unless you have something to compare it to. The first step is to know your rate of return (find yours at www.showmethereturn.ca)

and then compare your actual return to an appropriate benchmark. *Most investors do not know the rate of return they're earning, let alone how it compares with the appropriate benchmark. Check your performance against a benchmark at www.showmethebenchmark.ca.*

TAX: Income tax is our biggest expense. *We pay almost as much in tax as for all our other expenses combined.* Most investors miss opportunities to minimize their income tax bill.

# Conclusion

In his book *Play the Ball Where the Monkey Drops It*, Gregory Jones recounts how an acquaintance played one of the first rounds on a new golf course that had just opened at the Bombay Gold Club in India. It was a first-class course and it had every amenity. The club management had planned for everything, except for one thing—the monkeys. The problem was that often, as soon as a golfer took a shot, a monkey would jump down from the trees and grab the ball and carry it for a short distance before dropping it. Management tried everything to get rid of the monkeys and even had caddies throw balls on the ground under the trees where the monkeys sat in the hope that they would chase the caddies' golf balls instead of the golfers'. But nothing seemed to work. In any event, a few months later the golfer came back to the club to play again. In the clubhouse, he noticed that another rule had been recently added to the list: "Play the ball where the monkey drops it."

Perhaps this is the most important "rule" for retirement. After you've played by the rules and done everything you can, it is now time to accept reality and play from where you are today. You cannot go back and change your past. You can only go forward. You have to start playing from where you are today and make the best of your situation, whatever it may be.

# Acknowledgements

I dedicate this book to my wife, Paulette, who continually provides the care and support that enables me to put in the long hours necessary for success in any endeavour. Thank you, as well, to my sister Beverley, who helped type the first draft of the manuscript. —W.M.

Thank you to my sisters, Dorothy Lewis, Susan Hawkins, and Nancy Hawkins, who helped make this book relevant to the readers for whom it was intended. I also want to dedicate this book to the memory of my father, Joe Hawkins, who passed away just before his 94th birthday. Observing how he lived his life provided me with many valuable insights. My father's successful retirement was based on common sense, not on complex financial spreadsheets.—K.H.

We would like to thank our editor, Laurie Coulter. We also want to thank the many people at HarperCollins for their support of this book, including Brad Wilson, Allegra Robinson, Sharon Kish, and Deanna McFadden. And we thank our agent, Don Bastian, for his insight.

# Online Resources

## Part 1: Understand How Retirement Is Evolving

Boomernet—The Baby Boomers' Surfing Center
*www.boomernet.com*

Boomers International—World Wide Community for the Baby Boomer Generation
*www.boomersint.org*

Aging Hipsters—The Baby Boomer Generation
*www.aginghipsters.com/*

Senior Journal
*www.seniorjournal.com*

Seniors Canada
*www.seniors.gc.ca*

Seniors' Information Ontario
*www.seniorsinfo.ca*

Senior Years
*www.senioryears.com*

50Plus.com
*www.fifty-plus.net/*

Mature Resources
*www.matureresources.org*

Third Age
*www.thirdage.com*

## Part 2: Think about the Retirement Plan that's Right for You

"When Will I Die?" life expectancy calculator
*www.canadianbusiness.com/my_money/planning/retirement_rrsp/life_expectancy/tool.jsp*

MSN Money life expectancy calculator
*www.moneycentral.msn.com/investor/calcs/n_expect/main.asp*

Realage—Live Life to the Fullest
*www.realage.com/*

Pre-Retirement Planning Guide (Designed for U.S. residents; however, the non-financial aspects of planning should apply to Canadians as well.)
*www.goer.state.ny.us/train/onlinelearning/pr/lessonSub1.html*

Are You Ready for Retirement?
*www.up4retirement.com/*

Authentic Happiness—University of Pennsylvania Positive Psychology Center
*www.authentichappiness.sas.upenn.edu*

Canadian Wellness
*www.canadianwellness.com/*

Health Canada
*www.hc-sc.gc.ca/*

Canadian Health Network
*www.canadian-health-network.ca*
The Care Guide
*www.thecareguide.com*
Canadian Cancer Society
*www.cancer.ca/*
Canadian Heart and Stroke Foundation
*www.heartandstroke.com/*

## GENERAL TOPICS
House and Home/Retirement Homes
*www.retirementhomes.com*
*www.topretirements.com/Ebookdownloadguest.html*
Travelling and Living Abroad
*www.voyage.gc.ca*
Volunteering
*www.imaginecanada.ca*
*www.new.volunteer.ca*
*www.charityvillage.com*
Work and Retirement
*www.theskillsmatch.ca*
*www.retiredworker.ca*

## Part 3: Calculate Your Cost of Living in Retirement
Canada Revenue Agency
*www.cra-arc.gc.ca*
The Simple Living Network
*www.simpleliving.net*
Simple Debt-Free Living
*www.simpledebtfreeliving.com/*
Frugality Forum
*www.frugality.ca*
Choose to Save
*www.choosetosave.org*

## Part 4: Calculate Your Retirement Income
Canadian Government Retirement (information on CPP and Old Age Security
programs and how to apply for them)
*www.servicecanada.gc.ca/en/lifeevents/retirement.shtml*
Service Canada (information on the benefit programs and how to apply for them)
*www.rhdsc.gc.ca/en/isp/pub/oas/lis/listoc.shtml*

## PROVINCIAL WEBSITES

Alberta

*www.seniors.gov.ab.ca/financial_assistance/seniors_benefit/index.asp*

British Columbia

*www.cserv.gov.bc.ca/seniors/*

Manitoba

*www.gov.mb.ca/fs/assistance/55plus.html*

New Brunswick Services

*www.gnb.ca/0017/seniors/SeniorsGuide-e.pdf*

Newfoundland

*www.fin.gov.nl.ca/fin/taxcreditsprogs-lowsenr.html*

Northwest Territories

*www.hlthss.gov.nt.ca/seniors/default.asp*

Nova Scotia

*www.gov.ns.ca/scs/services.asp*

Ontario

*www.citizenship.gov.on.ca/seniors/english/programs/seniorsguide/*

Prince Edward Island

*www.gov.pe.ca/infopei/index.php3?number=16199&lang*

Saskatchewan

*www.cr.gov.sk.ca/seniors/*

Yukon

*www.housing.yk.ca/services/seniors.html*

## RETIREMENT AND FINANCIAL CALCULATORS

CCH Financial Planning Toolkit (Although geared to U.S. residents, many are applicable to Canadians as well.)

*www.finance.cch.com/tools/calcs.asp*

SeclonLogic Inc.

*www.seclonlogic.com/demo/default.asp*

Morningstar Retirement Planning Calculator

*www.morningstar.ca/globalhome/rrspplanner/index.asp*

## RISK AND INSURANCE

Canadian Life and Health Insurance Association

*www.clhia.ca*

Health Insurance Quotes

*www.healthquotes.ca/*

## Part 5: Follow a Simple and Sensible Investment Process

### FINANCIAL AND INVESTMENT INFORMATION AND EDUCATION

Toronto Stock Exchange

*www.tsx.com*

Financial Webring Forum (Chat room and discussion group on personal finance and investing in Canada. A good place to ask questions; many knowledgeable people will respond.)
*www.financialwebring.org/forum*
Choose to Save
*www.choosetosave.org/resources/*
Globe Investor
*www.globeinvestor.com/*
Sympatico Finance
*www.finance.sympatico.msn.ca/*
Investopedia
*www.investopedia.com*
Investor Education Fund (Ontario Securities Commission website covering all the basics of personal finance and investing)
*www.investored.ca/en/Pages/default.aspx*
Securities and Exchange Commission Online Publications for Investors (Although targeted at U.S. residents, much of it applies to Canadians as well.)
*www.sec.gov/investor/pubs_subject.shtml#ins_varann*

## BENCHMARKING AND INDEX PROVIDERS
Show Me the Benchmark (allows investors to calculate a customized benchmark rate of return over any period of time)
*www.showmethebenchmark.com*
Investment Performance Analysis
*www.andreassteiner.net/performanceanalysis/?Performance:Benchmarking*
MSCI Barra Indices (MSCI Barra is the leading supplier of global equity indexes used throughout the investing world. This site provides methodology and information about their indexes.)
*www.mscibarra.com/products/indices/*
Standard & Poor's (Standard and Poor's is the leading provider of equity indexes in North America. They provide the equity indices for the Toronto Stock Exchange. This site provides methodology and information about their indexes.)
*www2.standardandpoors.com*

## Part 6: Construct a Solid Investment Portfolio
### EXCHANGE TRADED FUNDS
iShares (provides information and strategy on iShares, the family of exchange traded funds based on Canadian stocks, of Barclays Global Investors Canada Limited)
*www.ishares.ca*
### MUTUAL FUNDS
Morningstar
*www.morningstar.ca*
Globefund (Part of *The Globe and Mail*'s online services. Provides information on Canadian mutual funds.)
*www.globefund.com*

### REVERSE MORTGAGES

Canadian Home Income Plan (site of the leading provider of reverse mortgages in
Canada)
*www.chip.ca*

## Part 7: Monitor and Manage Your Investments Wisely

How to Avoid Investment Frauds and Scams (online brochure sponsored by the B.C.
Securities Commission)
*www.bcsc.bc.ca/uploadedFiles/CSA_Seniors-Protect.pdf*
Investment Counsel Association of Canada (helps users to find investment
counsellors and provides a checklist of what to look for when hiring one)
*www.investmentcounsel.org*

### GENERAL RESEARCH ON ISSUES OF RETIREMENT AND RELATED SUBJECTS

Canadian Social Research Links
*www.canadiansocialresearch.net/seniors.htm*
Wiser Women's Institute for a Secure Retirement
*www.wiserwomen.org*
AARP Policy and Research (AARP is the leading advocacy group for seniors in the
U.S. This website contains their research and public policy statements.)
*www.aarp.org/research/*
Seniors and Baby Boomers Markets World Wide
*www.thematuremarket.com*
Center for Retirement Research at Boston College
*crr.bc.edu/*
Fidelity Research Institute (Fidelity is the largest mutual fund company in the world.
This site contains research in investing and personal finance, with particular
emphasis on retirement funding.)
*www.fidelityresearchinstitute.com*
Employee Benefit Research Institute
*www.ebri.org/*
Retirement Research Center—University of Michigan
*www.mrrc.isr.umich.edu/*
Pension Research Council—Wharton University of Pennsylvania
*www.pensionresearchcouncil.org/*
Retirement Reports and Articles by Prudential
*www.prudential.com/view/page/13175*
Statistics Canada Publications
*www.dsp-psd.communication.gc.ca/Collection/Statcan/index-e.html*
Investment News Retirement Center
*www.investmentnews.com/apps/pbcs.dll/section?category=RetirementCenter*
Service Canada Pension Plan—Related Sites
*www.hrsdc.gc.ca/en/isp/common/relatedsites.shtml*

# Bibliography

Adler, Jerry. "The Boomer Files," *Newsweek*. November 14, 2005.

Ameriks, John, Nestor, Robert, and Utkus, Stephan. *Expectations for Retirement: A Survey of Retirement Investors.* The Vanguard Center for Retirement Research, November 2004.

Ameriks, John, Fergusson, Holly, Madamba, Anna, and Utkus, Stephan. *Six Paths to Retirement.* The Vanguard Center for Retirement Research, Volume 26, January 2007.

Ameriprise Financial. *The New Retirement Landscape.* January 2006.

Anthony, Mitch. *The New Retirementality: Planning Your Life and Living Your Dreams ... at Any Age You Want.* Chicago: Dearborn Financial Publishing Inc., 2001.

Arnott, Robert, and Casscells, Anne. *Demographics and Capital Market Returns,* March/April 2003.

BMO Financial Group. *BMO Retirement Trends Study—Overview.* Toronto, 2006.

Belanger, Alain, Martel, Laurent, and Caron-Malenfant, Eric. *Population Projections for Canada, Provinces and Territories 2005–2031.* Statistics Canada Catalogue No. 91–520-XIE, 2005.

Bender, Keith A., and Jivan, Natalia A. *What Makes Retirees Happy?* An Issue in Brief, Center for Retirement Research at Boston College, Number 28, February 2005.

Benefits Canada. *Putting a Face on CAP Members.* Special Report on CAP Members, Benefits Canada, November 2006.

Bernicke, Ty. "Reality Retirement Planning: A New Paradigm for an Old Science." *Journal of Financial Planning,* June 2005.

Bolles, Richard, and Nelson, John. *What Color Is Your Parachute?—For Retirement,* Berkeley: Ten Speed Press, 2007.

Brock, Fred. *Retire on Less than You Think: The New York Times Guide to Planning Your Financial Future.* New York: Times Books, Henry Holt and Company, 2004.

Brown, S. Kathi. *Impact of Stock Market Decline on 50–70-Year-Old Investors.* AARP, 2002.

CMHC. *2001 Census Housing Series: Issue 9 Revised. The Housing Conditions of Canada's Seniors,* Research Highlight. Canadian Housing and Mortgage Corporation, April 2005.

CMHC. *2001 Census Housing Series: Issue 10. Aging, Residential Mobility and Housing Choices,* Research Highlight. Canadian Housing and Mortgage Corporation, February 2006.

CSA. *Principal-Protected Notes.* Canadian Securities Administrators' Notice 46–303.

Calvo, Esteban. *Does Working Longer Make People Healthier and Happier?* An Issue in Brief, Center for Retirement Research, Boston College, February 2006.

Canadian Securities Institute. *Canadian Insurance Course,* Volumes 1 & 2. Toronto: CSI Publishing, 2004.

Canadian Securities Institute. *Professional Financial Planning Course,* Volumes 1 & 2. Toronto: CSI Publishing, 2001.

Carlson, Robert. *The New Rules of Retirement: Strategies for a Secure Future.* Hoboken, NJ: John Wiley & Sons Inc., 2005.

Chawla, Raj K. *Change in Expenditure Patterns of Older Households in Canada, 1982–2003.* 29th General Conference of The International Association for Research in Income and Wealth, Joensuu, Finland, August 20–26, 2006.

Clark, Warren. *What Do Seniors Spend on Housing?* Canadian Social Trends, Statistics Canada, Catalogue No. 11–008, Autumn 2005.

Coile, Courtney, and Milligan, Kevin. *What Happens to Household Portfolios after Retirement?* An Issue in Brief, Center for Retirement Research, Boston College, November 2006, No. 56.

Congressional Budget Office. *Baby Boomers' Retirement Prospects: An Overview.* The Congress of the United States, November 2003.

Cooper, Sherry. *The New Retirement: How It Will Change Our Future.* Toronto: Penguin Group, 2008.

Darlin, Damon. "A Contrarian View: Save Less, Retire with Enough." *The New York Times,* January 27, 2007.

DeCaen, Vincent, and Folk, Levi. *Principal-Protected Notes: How, Why and When.* Fund Library Research Group, May 18, 2005.

Eisenberg, Lee. *The Number: A Completely Different Way to Think about the Rest of Your Life.* New York: Free Press, 2006.

Farrell, Diane, Ghai, Sacha, and Shavers, Tim. "The Demographic Deficit: How Aging Will Reduce Global Wealth." *The McKinsey Quarterly,* March 2005.

Go, Erwin. *Year 2006 in Review. IFIC's Annual Review of the Canadian Mutual Fund Industries Statistics.* The Investment Funds Institute of Canada, 2007.

Hamilton, Clive. *Downshifting in Britain: A Sea-Change in Pursuit of Happiness.* The Australia Institute, Discussion Paper Number 58, November 2003.

Hamilton, Clive, and Mail, Elizabeth. *Downshifting in Australia: A Sea-Change in Pursuit of Happiness.* The Australia Institute, Discussion Paper Number 50, January 2003.

Health Canada. *Canada's Aging Population,* Government of Canada.

Helman, Ruth, Copeland, Craig, and Vanderhei, Jack. *Will More of Us Be Working Forever? The 2006 Retirement Confidence Survey.* Issue Brief No. 292 Employee Benefit Research Institute, April 2006.

Hovanec, Margret, and Shilton, Elizebeth. *Redefining Retirement: New Realities for Boomer Women.* Toronto: Second Story Press, 2007.

Hutchens, Robert. *Phased Retirement: Problems and Prospects.* An Issue in Brief, Center for Retirement Research, Boston College, February 2007.

Investor Education Fund. *An Analysis of Trends in the Defined Contribution Market in Canada.* May 15, 2003.

Khorana, Ajay, Servaes, Henri, and Tufano, Peter. *Mutual Fund Fees Around the World.* Draft: May 1, 2007.

Lin, Jane. *The Housing Transitions of Seniors.* Canadian Social Trends, Statistics Canada, Catalogue No. 11–008, Winter 2005.

Lovett-Reid, Patricia, and Verney, Jonathan. *Live Well, Retire Well: Strategies for a Rich Life and a Richer Retirement.* Toronto: Key Porter Books Limited, 2006.

MacKenzie, Warren A. *The Unbiased Advisor: 108 Ways to Make Money, Achieve Financial Health and Avoid Costly Investment Mistakes.* Toronto: HarperCollins Publishers Ltd, 2007.

Macunovich, Diane J. *The Baby Boomers.* Columbia University, October 2000.

McCarthy, Ed. "The Evolution of Retirement Planning." *Journal of Financial Planning,* May 2002.

Morissette, Rene, and Zhang, Xuelin. *Revisiting Wealth Inequality.* Statistics Canada Perspectives on Labour and Income, Volume 7, Number 12, Catalogue No. 75–001-XIE, December 2006.

National Advisory Council on Aging. *Aging in Poverty in Canada: Seniors on the Margins,* Government of Canada.

National Advisory Council on Aging. *Seniors in Canada 2006 Report Card,* Government of Canada.

National Union Research. *A Brief History of Pensions in Canada.* Pensions Backgrounder #2, National Union of Public and General Employees, March 2007.

National Union Research. *No Pension Panic- The Real Pension Crisis, It's All about Coverage—Not Funding.* National Union of Public and General Employees, November 2006.

National Union Research. *Pensions Are Important.* Pensions Backgrounder #1, National Union of Public and General Employees, March 2007.

Pape, Gordon. *The Retirement Time Bomb: How to Achieve Financial Independence in a Changing World.* Toronto: Penguin Group, 2006.

Prudential. *Behavioral Risk in the Retirement Red Zone.* Prudential Financial's Four Pillars of Retirement Series, April 2007.

RE/MAX. *Recreational Property Report.* May 2007.

Robinson, Charles D. "A Phased-Income Approach to Retirement Withdrawals: A New Paradigm for a More Affluent Retirement." *Journal of Financial Planning,* March 2007.

Roper, A.S.W. *Baby Boomers Envision Retirement II: Survey of Baby Boomers' Expectations for Retirement.* AARP, May 2004.

SEI Investments. *DC Pension Plan Members: Psychographic Profiles.* SEI Investments, November 2004.

SOM. *National Survey on Retirement—5th edition.* Desjardins Financial Security, October 2006

Schellenberg, Grant, Turcotte, Martin, and Rem, Bali. *What Makes Retirement Enjoyable.* Canadian Social Trends, Statistics Canada Catalogue No. 11–008, Autumn 2005.

Singh, Mohindar. "The Myths of Aging." *Expressions, Bulletin of the National Advisory Council on Aging,* Volume 16, Number 2, Spring 2003.

Society of Actuaries, *Post Retirement Risks: Changing Needs and Resources*

Society of Actuaries. *Report of Findings: 2005 Risks and Process of Retirement Survey,* March 2006.

Statistics Canada. *Health at Older Ages.* Health Reports Special Issue, Supplement to
   Volume 16, Catalogue No. 82–003, February 2006.
Statistics Canada. *Life Tables, Canada, Provinces and Territories, 2000 to 2002.*
   Catalogue No. 84–537-XIE July 2006.
Statistics Canada. *Portrait of the Canadain Population in 2006, 2006 Census—
   Population and Dwelling Counts, 2006 Census,* Statistics Canada, Catalogue No.
   97–550-XIE, March 2007.
Statistics Canada. *Report on the Demographic Situation in Canada 2003 and 2004.*
   Catalogue No. 91–209-XIE, June 2006.
Statistics Canada. *The Wealth of Canadians: An Overview of the Results of the Survey
   of Financial Security 2005.* Pension and Wealth Research Paper Series, Statistics
   Canada, Catalogue No. 13F0026MIE—No. 001, December 2006.
Statistics Canada. *Women and Men in Canada: A Statistical Glance 2003 Edition*
Strategic Counsel. The. "State of the Baby Boomers." A Report to *The Globe and Mail,*
   *The Globe and Mail,* June 2006.
Tal, Benjamin. *Retirement: Ready or Not?,* CIBC World Markets, February 6, 2007.
Turcotte, Martin and Schellenberg, Grant. *A Portrait of Seniors in Canada.* Statistics
   Canada Catalogue no. 89–519-XIE, February 2007.
Van Harlow, W. *The Equity You Live In: The Home as a Retirement Savings and Income
   Option.* Fidelity Research Institute, February 2007.
Van Harlow, W and Feinschreiber, Steven. *Beyond Conventional Wisdom: New
   Strategies for Lifetime Income.* Fidelity Research Institute, September 26, 2006.

# Index

*Play the Ball Where the Monkey Drops It*
(Jones), 3–4
portfolios
active vs. passive management, 149–51
asset allocation, 14, 150–51
constructing, 175–202
keeping simple, 153–54, 182–83, 208, 215
managing, 205–20
managing one's own, 15, 215–18
monitoring performance, 153–59
passive management, 188
proper diversification, 185–87
principal, drawing down, 13–14, 113, 195–98
principal-protected notes (PPNs), 201–2
public policy, potential effect on retirement
savings, 128

quality of life, vs. standard of living, 2–3, 12,
15–16, 27–31, 42
Quebec Pension Plan (QPP), 85, 91–93

Ram, Bali, 28–29
re-careering, 40
recreational properties, 50
recre-retirement, 50, 118
Registered Retirement Income Funds (RRIFs),
99–101
effect of rate of return, 100–101
minimum withdrawals, 100
taxation of withdrawals, 14, 99, 101, 102–3,
168–71
withdrawals from, 14–15
Registered Retirement Savings Plans (RRSPs),
85
converting to RRIFs, 99–101
savings outside of, 101–4
taxation of withdrawals, 14, 168–71
transferring pension benefits into, 97
vs. non-registered accounts, 102
withdrawals from, 14–15
retirees
confidence in finances, 21
"work and play," 41
retirement
anxiety over, 20–22, 86
baby boomers' expectations of, 8, 11–12
changing perceptions of, 7–9, 11–12
creating a vision for, 25

early, 29, 31, 41, 42, 107–8
effect of preparation on well-being, 29, 30
estimated length of, 53–56
expenses in early years, 61–70
factors affecting well-being, 27–31
goals for, 3
involuntary, 12, 28, 32, 39
lifestyle issues, 3, 11, 17–22, 29, 30, 33, 36,
39, 61–62, 65, 77
making transition to, 39–45
myths and misconceptions, 1–3, 11–16, 215
phased-in, 40, 43–46, 109
saving for, 18–20
timing of, 12, 29, 106–10
undue focus on standard of living, 2–3, 12,
15–16
working during, 11, 30, 35, 39–43, 109
retirement communities, 50, 118–19
retirement homes, generation gaps within,
50–51
retirement income. *See also* investment
income, Registered Retirement Income
Funds (RRIFs)
company pension plans, 18, 27, 40, 95–98,
177
deferral of, 92–93, 106–7
estimating, 85–87
government entitlement programs, 18,
85–87, 89–94
retirement living, trends in, 49–52, 118–19
retirement planning
relationship to financial security, 19–20
retirement savings, drawing down of,
13–14, 113
"return-ment," 40, 42
reverse mortgages, 198–99
risk tolerance questionnaires, 141
Royal LePage, 50

saving money
after retirement, 63, 76, 195–202
obstacles, 18–20
outside of RRSPs, 101–4
rate expected to decline, 113
Schellenberg, Grant, 28–29
segregated funds, 164–66
Selnow, Gary, 18–19
"sinking" funds, 66